Rev. Mose-
5601 Crabapple Ct
968·9076

# The Senior Adult Years

# THE SENIOR ADULT YEARS

Carroll B. Freeman

BROADMAN PRESS
Nashville, Tennessee

4254-21

ISBN: 0-8054-5421-7

Dewey Decimal Classification: 155.67
Subject heading: ELDERLY
Library of Congress Catalog Card Number: 79-51137
Printed in the United States of America

# Dedicated

**to my parents**
Father—Riley L. Freeman (1892-1953)
Mother—Mary Bessford Reynolds Freeman (1894-     )

In 1953 my father became seriously ill with a failing heart and was admitted to a hospital for the first and last time in his life. An awareness of his last days must have prompted him to speak in a very special way to his three sons. He wanted to remind us of something that was very important to him. Very quietly he said, "Do you remember what our Lord said as he hung on the cross?" He paused, then continued, "Jesus said, 'Behold thy mother!' " No elaboration was necessary and I do not remember that any further word was spoken. It was a sacred moment as the deepest concern of a great Christian father was indelibly etched in our minds and hearts.

# Acknowledgments

I am indebted to a host of helpers who have made this book possible. Hellon my wife has loved, encouraged, typed, and aided in research. Laura Morrison, an assistant, has provided a wide range of assistance that has proven to be extremely valuable as the responsibilities of everyday work and writing efforts were woven together. The most sophisticated slave labor that the world has ever known—beloved doctoral students have provided a wealth of research and feedback. Many other students have helped, but I remember four who have done extensive research—Beth Strange, Ken Gilburth, William Hanks, and Rick Lance. Deepest gratitude is felt and expressed for the opportunity, direction, editing, and friendship provided by Horace Kerr, supervisor of the Senior Adult Section of the Baptist Sunday School Board; Lee Sizemore, my editor and friend; and a host of senior adults who have enriched my life.

# Preface

The primary purpose of this book is to portray a realistic description of senior adults from a Christo-psychological perspective. The word *realistic* implies an appraisal of the psychological life of senior adults that is as free from bias as possible.

I have been trained in psychopathology and in a religious orientation that has placed much emphasis on sin. Evidently, certain advantages are derived from recognizing sickness, ugliness, and aberrant behavior. However, we desperately need criteria of beauty and holiness ever before us to make certain that when we call something ugly or sinful we are justified in doing so. Health, beauty, and holiness need criteria of destructiveness and sickness to further clarify them. Thus, we need to assess the weaknesses as well as the strengths and potentialities of aging. Great dangers are inherent in extremes in either direction. If we maximize the needs and trauma of aging, we will surely run in that direction as if to fulfill prophecy. If we glorify aging we may develop a lack of sensitivity to the fundamental needs that must be met for the aged to reach his full potential. A vital balance is necessary if we are to avoid the pitfalls that are beneath both our desperate needs to help and the subtle "put down" of our effusive compliments and false encouragement. We are slowly passing through the youth-cult stage of our present culture. An overcorrection may result from unrealistic assessments of the negative or positive aspects of becoming senior adults. It is not likely, but imagine a senior adult-cult oriented society. Certainly we need to rush to the high side of the listing ship, but we need to be careful or risk the possibility of a "Poseidon Adventure." We may sink the ship. A type of grandiosity or gerontophilia may be created that fosters bitterness and resistance from the other age groups within society. Age will be set upon and she will be outnumbered. Then, in 2050 someone will say, "Look how mistreated are our older Americans."

I am suggesting that a realistic view of aging will serve as a monitor that guides in the selection and interpretation of material presented in the following pages. As Clark Tibbitts, noted gerontologist and author, has said, aging people can play positive roles through which they can make valuable contributions to society. Tibbitts, in his *Handbook on Social Gerontology,* calls for a new concept of aging—one that gives recognition to the positive as well as the negative aspects of maturation.

Specific audiences were kept in mind as this book on understanding senior adults was written. The first is the large and growing group of church leaders who work either as general staff persons or as the beginning group of specialists in aging at the local church level. At present these specialists are limited in number. However, an evident shift is seen from a preoccupation with declining numbers of youth to an emphasis on specialized ministry to the growing population of seniors. The second audience is college and graduate students who have found that people, on the average, are getting older and thus, increased occupational opportunities to work beside and for them are available. The third group is the senior adults themselves. We may find that they are a receptive and appreciative audience. The fourth audience in mind is the children of senior adults. A popular but untrue notion is that noncaring children are in the majority. The material in the following pages may help them gain new perspectives of their parents and free them from the uncertainties and anxieties that are so prevalent.

# Contents

Introduction . . . . . . . . . . . . . . . . . . . . . . . . . . . . . . . . . . . . . . . . . . . .  13

**Chapter 1 Behold Thy Mother** . . . . . . . . . . . . . . . . . . . . . . . . . . . . .  17

Made in the image of God
Obligation and gratitude
Honoring senior adults
A social problem
Our greatest untapped resource
Prudential wisdom
A Christian psychology of aging?

**Chapter 2 Figures Don't Lie: Demographics and
other Interesting Statistics** . . . . . . . . . . . . . . . . . . . . . . . . . . . . .  28

Life expectancy trends
Ratio to total U.S. population
Sex ratios
Comparison to other countries
Racial population ratios
Education
Residential distribution
Employment
Dependency ratio
Health facts

**Chapter 3 Psychological Functions** ........................ 42

Intelligence and the Senior Adult
The Intelligence-quotient (I.Q.)
Correcting early tests of senior adults
A generation gap
Distance from death
Biased I.Q. tests
A new description of intelligence
Summary
Sensory Functions and the Senior Adult ................... 49
Vision
Hearing
Taste and smell
Learning and Senior Adults ........................... 55
Physical factors in senior adult learning
Psychological factors in senior adult learning
Pedagogy, andragogy, and geriogogy
Senior adults and Christian education
Memory ............................................... 62
Attitudes............................................. 67
Attitudes about death
Attitudes about grandparenthood
Miscellaneous attitudes and perceptions
Sensorimotor Skills and Aging......................... 74
Summary and Conclusions ............................. 75

**Chapter 4 Psychological Needs**........................... 78

The Need to be Socially Involved....................... 80
The need and theology
Continued number and variety of relationships needed
The quality of social involvements
Dimensions of social involvements
Five Christian principles for social involvements
Knownness *Versus* Anonymity
Integrity *Versus* Deceit and Duplicity
Caring *Versus* Using

Responsibility *Versus* Irresponsibility
Durability *Versus* Separation and Estrangement
The Love Need ....................................... 104
The Need to Be Worthwhile to Self and Others............. 110
    Being useful
    The will to meaning
    A Christian interpretation
    Other Lists of Needs


**Chapter 5 Psychological Adjustments and Development** ....... 121

Adjustment ......................................... 121
    Defintion of adjustment
    Stress and adjustment
    Crises and adjustment
Adjustment Shocks ................................... 129
    Unemployment
    Loss of income and possessions
    Loss of status
    Loss of selfhood
    Trends
    The gift of retirement
    A time to retire
    Loss of health
    Loss of independence
    Too much help?
    Cultural or biological?
    Independence related to many losses
    Destructive independence
    A portrait of dependency (loss of surroundings)
    Dependency and anger
    Loss of significant others
    Facing dying and death
    Facing ageism
    Definition of "ageism"
    Social change and ageism
    Myths

Development (Adjustment and Beyond) ................... 148
   Aging as development
   Popular theories of successful aging
   Theory of disengagement
   Activity theory
   Developmental theory
   Other theories
   Havighurst's proposed adjustment tasks
   Motivation and personality development
   Conflict model
   Fulfillment model
   Consistency model
   A Christian model
   Uphill and downhill development
   Development of characteristic tendencies
   Potential for the development of life's greatest values

**Chapter 6 Psychological Disorders** ......................... 164

   Questions?
   Side effects
   Hope!
Etiology (Study of Causes) ................................ 165
   Physiological cause
   Biochemical cause
   Psychodymanic cause
   Genetic cause
Somatogenic Psychological Disorders ...................... 169
   Organic brain syndrome
   Symptoms
   Mental retardation of senior adults
   Psychogenic Psychological and Physical Disorders .......... 173
      Depression
      Suicide
      Manic behavior
      Paranoid reactions
      Mind over body disorders
      Situational disturbances

Drug abuse and alcoholism
Other disorders
Disorders and Views of God ............................ 185

**Chapter 7. Psychological Implications** ...................... 187

You caused it!
We caused it!
We can all win!
Changed Attitudes ..................................... 190
Mending Fences and Finding Forgiveness ................. 192
New proclamation fence posts
Educational alterations
Mend the fences together
Oiling the hinges
Jerusalem was mentioned first
Faith That Old Age May Be the Most Beautiful Time of Life . 201
Preparation for Aging ................................. 202

## List of Tables

1. Average Life Expectancy in the United States at Birth
   and at Age 65 from 1900-1970 ......................... 29

2. Number of Women Compared to 100 Males in Particular
   Age Groupings for Selected Years ..................... 31

3. Life Expectancy ...................................... 32

4. Size of Ethnic Groups ................................ 33

5. Projections of Future Educational Levels of the 65+
   Population in the United States from 1975-1990 .......... 35

6. The Population and Percentage Increase of the 65+
   Group in Ten States with Largest Concentration: 1970 ..... 37

7. Percentage of the Elderly Participating in the Labor
   Force by Age and Sex, 1940 through 1975 ............... 38

8. Dependency Ratios for the 65+ Age Group in the
   United States: 1930-2050 .............................. 39

9. Thurstone's Primary Mental Abilities and Examples of
   Their Meaning ...................................... 44

10. The Stress of Adjusting to Change ........................ 124

11. Median Schooling of Older Labor Force Members as
    Percentage of Median of Younger Members
    (1959 and 1969) ...................................... 133

## List of Illustrations

1. Proportion of Words Recalled and Recognized Following
   Four Different Orienting Task Conditions ................ 66

2. Involvement of Other Age Groups Shown in Expanding
   Concentric Circles, Involvement of Senior Adults as
   Diminishing Concentric Circles ........................ 84

3. Maslow's Hierarchy of Needs ............................ 108

# Introduction

Any book needs to be well born. The time required in its preparation and reading is a tragic waste unless there is planned parenthood. Some works are like children born out of season while other works provide an exhilarating sense of fulfillment for their writers and information and inspiration for their readers. A first consideration is the background of the author. His education, training, experience, and especially certain motivational factors, should be adequate for the task. Also, the book should flow from a sense of responsibility for life with a clear purpose in mind. This purpose can only be realized as specific audiences are targeted through meeting needs of interest and information.

A book well born should have Christ as its life-giver. Thus, the sub-title, *A Christian Psychology of Aging,* is appropriate. A psychology of aging should be written from this Person orientation. To be a better book, the material should be comprehensive as to psychological functions and written in a simple but challenging style. We purport that this book meets these requisites and does so with a realistic yet positive view of aging.

## Background of the Author

In *The Art of Understanding Your Mate,* Cecil Osborne tells of a young, unmarried psychologist who wrote a book and titled it, *Ten Commandments for Parents.* After marriage, a baby, and several years, a revision appeared with a new title, *Ten Suggestions for Parents.* Again, several years later and after the arrival of the fourth child, he opted for another revision with the title, *Ten Possible Hints for Parents.*[1] It may appear that I am somewhat presumptuous in writing about senior adults when I am not considered one of the crowd, chronologically! Since the title. "Senior Adult" may be one of honor and signifies

13

much more than a specific chronological age, I may be privileged to be one of them, even though I am only fifty years of age!

A great American humorist of the past said, "We are all ignorant— just ignorant in different places." The task of writing an acceptable text for a psychological understanding of senior adults has been complex and humbling. However, preparation for my participation in this venture began early in my life as I was nurtured by the older men and women who comprised the strong leadership of my home church. A large group of unusually gifted and dedicated senior adults virtually surrounded me. Dr. Wayne Todd, General William L. Clark, Dr. R. A. McLemore, and numerous others well known in Southern Baptist life, were nurtured in this same small church where senior adults were so prominent.

Fortunately, I married a lovely girl who had as her dearest friends many oldsters in the community. How many times have I heard about Mrs. Lee, Mr. Hood, Mr. and Mrs. Durfey, Mrs. McLemore, Mr. and Mrs. Vance, and on and on. Can you guess where she takes her Thanksgiving and Christmas baskets? Through the years we wondered, "Oh, what can we do to help make life more fulfilling to older people?" Dozens of plans and schemes (some grandiose) evolved and filled our dreams in exciting moments of sharing. If you do not want to work, be careful how you dream. You may find yourself pouring over books and articles and trying to put some beautiful experiences into words that will bring about a better understanding of the last third of earthly life.

My mother, who is eighty-five years of age, drives her own car, and lives alone, has provided a very personal experience of aging. The strengths, flaws, crises, and many of the issues and problems of aging are constantly near; as near as first person. Her strengths are a source of reveling, with the flaws and crises guiding me to a more realistic appraisal of aging in the life of this one individual. There is less than two blocks distance between my mother and my wife's grandmother, who is ninety-one years of age. She is almost blind, lives alone, and moves about with the help of a walker. She fell and broke her hip several years ago. She is alert and intelligent, a former teacher of the women's Bible class in the church mentioned earlier. There they are in my background, past and present, a panorama of aging covering one hundred and seventy-six years of life. Almost simultaneously they are seen, both old; both so different with common problems and characteristics—a living laboratory for a close, personal understanding of two senior adults.

God's providence, the national focus on senior adults, and my beginnings led me to write papers on aging at the master's level in seminary training. My first doctoral seminar paper was entitled, "Counseling the Elderly: A New Frontier for Pastoral Counseling." From that point on through the completion of doctoral work and beyond, psychology was vitally related to aging. My first intense clinical experience with senior adults was provided in Southeast Louisiana Hospital, a center for treatment, training, and research in acute psychological disorders. Dr. Carolyn Kitchin, a psychiatrist who (at this writing) is assistant commissioner of mental health for the state of Louisiana, assigned me the responsibility for leading group sessions composed largely of senior adults.

Those were exciting years that led eventually to a position with the Mississippi Council on Aging as an areawide coordinator of agencies on aging. This responsibility entailed a close working relationship with staff and senior adults in one of the nine original model projects in the United States. The cachement area for the model included three populous counties in southern Mississippi which bordered the Gulf of Mexico. Clinical gerontology, in its beginnings, demanded continual training. Studies at the University of Michigan, Mississippi State University, and in numerous local and regional seminars were essential if I were to contribute to this growing new science of aging.

A call came from New Orleans Baptist Theological Seminary: "Will you consider serving on our faculty in the area of psychology and counseling?" My yes was a halting reply because of my deep involvement in the field of aging. Interviews followed, and with reticence and uncertainty I answered no and later, yes. Out of this choice came opportunities to teach courses and seminars on aging for the New Orleans Baptist Theological Seminary and Mississippi State University. Other distinct contributions to my background have come via participation in the Southern Baptist Conference on Aging in 1974, project GIST (Gerontology in Seminary Training)—a project sponsored by the National Interfaith Coalition on Aging, and as a member of the Group on Aging of the Southern Baptist Convention Inter-Agency Council.

Please indulge me the pleasure of sharing one other area of background. From this area irrefutable evidence is offered as to the beauty and power potential of aging. It is derived from the opportunity to serve side by side with colleagues at New Orleans Baptist Theological Seminary who are senior adults and to see firsthand this potential being realized.

A grave responsibility is ours. Read on, and reach for a psychological understanding which may guide us in helping others and ourselves in becoming as beautiful as we were when God first thought of making us.

NOTES

[1]Cecil G. Osborne, *The Art of Understanding Your Mate* (Grand Rapids: Zondervan Publishing House, 1970), p. 116.

# 1

# Behold Thy Mother

"Now there stood by the cross of Jesus his mother, and his mother's sister, Mary the wife of Cleophas, and Mary Magdalene. When Jesus therefore saw his mother, and the disciple standing by, whom he loved, he saith unto his mother, Woman, behold thy son! Then saith he to the disciple, Behold thy mother! And from that hour that disciple took her unto his own home" (John 19:25-27).

Responsibility is possibly one of the most significant concepts in psychology. In a discussion of interpersonal relationships, a topic given attention elsewhere, this concept of responsibility will be dealt with in more detail. But it is appropriate to consider the "why" of responsibility in helping senior adults, especially in the matter of writing a book. It may appear obvious but that is an assumption that may find opposition in the writings of Ayn Rand and others.

If we could understand why we are responsible, then it appears reasonable that our perceptions of senior adults could be changed. Rather than the occasional provision of some type of help for the moment, you may be motivated toward a second order change—new perceptions, conceptualizations, and communication about the reality of our responsibility to our elders. This change may be more permanent. "Why?" is an essential, basic question. The "what" of responsibility is much more complex and will demand a psychological understanding of each individual. The "why responsible?" if answered, can provide direction and powerful motivation in fulfilling responsibility. Insights about how to be responsible should be implicit and, at times, explicit through this book. Several select reasons for this sense of responsibility will be briefly discussed.

17

## Made in the image of God

Theological debate swirls about this popular belief substantiated in God's Word. Regardless of how this phrase is interpreted or construed, intuition and revelation indicate that one should develop his Godlike qualities. One of the outstanding psychologists-philosophers, Erich Fromm, who is of dubious religious inclination, has written a provocative book titled, *And Ye Shall Be as Gods.* The scriptural account of Adam and Eve's beginnings bear out man's struggle to usurp God rather than to be increasingly like him. If you would know man's potential, look at God, especially as he is revealed in our Lord. If you would know the Lord, look at man's potential. Man is revealed through Christ and Christ may be revealed through man, at least by glimpses of man in his highest moments.

Responsibility is drawn to a burning focus at this point. Senior adults must be helped through all possible means to fulfill the image of God within them. The freedom of will, without shackling circumstances and dependencies, should be kept free indeed. The other-love potential rather than self-directed love must resemble the kind of love which was manifested in Christ. Other attributes of God serve as standards toward which men must strive as they live all their lives.

The idea of salvation as escape appears antithetical to the purpose of God's creation of man. Imagine, God made man so that he could be lost in order that he could be saved. No! The Creator made man for relationship—a mutuality that can only be fulfilled as man moves within the range of fellowship with his Maker. Of course, an experience of grace is essential, but this is only the beginning as man, through the exercise of the graces of God, desires his company, chooses him, and grows in his capacity for relationship with God.

This responsibility should be met in the development of those Godlike qualities of each individual that foster selfhood rather than a symbiotic attachment that is a losing and never finding of oneself. No apology is made for the foundational belief undergirding this book, that selfhood is only fully realized in Christ. According to Wayne E. Oates, professor of psychiatry at the University of Louisville, Christ is essential for selfhood. Christ's struggle to understand his heritage, vocation, and destiny is replicated in the life of every individual.[1] A sermon by the therapeutic preacher, John Claypool, "Claiming Your Place and Power," gave expression to this fulfillment of the image of God that surges within the life of each senior adult. Claypool vividly illustrates the individual's need to claim his place and power by relating a worship experience in an Episcopal church. The regular priest was absent and an older priest was there to present the message for the morning service. A young priest was tending to the rituals and had taken more time than necessary for this function and had encroached on the time allotted for the older priest. As the rituals progressed, the older man stood, approached the young associate, and whispered in his ear. The novice, obviously embarrassed, hastily completed his part of the service. When the older priest arose to speak, he explained that he had prepared a message from God for that hour and he was claiming his place and the power necessary for its delivery.

At first, Claypool, the guest, questioned the propriety of such an act. But reflecting upon the life of Christ, he found that the crowds had different expectations for Christ. They wanted stones converted to bread, miraculous acrobatics demonstrated, and kingdom leadership initiated. He did not comply to a single request, but rather claimed his unique place and power. This was an expression of the unique Son of God and was a fulfillment of the image of God within Him.[2]

## Obligation and gratitude

Obligation, an element of responsibility, is vital in many interpersonal relationships. Obligation may be defined as the condition of being in debt for a favor, service, or such. Obligation for many acts of kindness, the adherence to timeless values, and a parental sense which has blessed successive generations, as well as their own, inspires a sense of responsibility to senior adults. Of course, great and good things have been produced by youth as well as age, but many senior adults were at one time these noble youths to whom obligation is now due. It would seem that a prime obligation of youth is to understand senior adults—more importantly to experience empathy for them. Yet, in doing so, blessings follow—in attempting to meet an obligation one is again blessed.

To be responsible for gratitude appears paradoxical. This is only when freedom and responsibility are not properly understood. If responsibility is viewed as coercion in relation to gratitude, then something other than thankfulness would be the result. The desire and the ability to respond with gratitude to senior adults is not alien to Scripture. The Bible is filled with commands to express gratitude. A notable example is blind Bartimaeus. An extraordinary example of this combination of debt and gratitude is expressed in the preface of *Why Survive?* a Pulitzer Prize winning book (1975) written by Robert N. Butler, psychiatrist and director of the new National Institute on Aging of the National Institutes of Health. Butler shared in "A Personal Note" the following:

What leads a physician to gerontology? A psychiatrist? A young practitioner did not find in his medical or clinical training in the 1950s—any more than today—much knowledge, sympathy, or understanding of the mental and physical needs of the elderly; but my childhood compelled this interest.

My grandparents reared me from infancy. My parents separated shortly after my birth, and when I was eleven months old, my mother brought me to live with her parents in Vineland, New Jersey, where my grandfather, then in his seventies, was a gentleman chicken farmer. I remember his blue overalls, his lined face and abundant white hair. He was my close friend and my teacher. Together we rose at 4 A.M. each day to feed chickens, candle eggs, grow oats, and tend to the sick chickens in the "hospital" at one end of the chicken house. He would tell me of his younger days in Oklahoma and I would listen eagerly.

He disappeared suddenly when I was seven. I came back from a visit to a neighbor and he was gone. It made no sense. My grandmother said he went to visit relatives in Oklahoma—but he had not told me anything about the trip. With time, I realized I was never going to see him again. Dismay turned to fright and then to grief. I knew before they told me that he was dead.

Why? Why had he died? Why did people die? There was no talk, no funeral, only a "protective" silence that was more confusing than shared sorrow. I felt my silent way through a child's questions and a child's answers. Mostly, of course, I wanted to bring him back. Surely someone could arrange it. Everyone ought to live forever. No, that clearly would make for too many problems: old people would accumulate in hordes and the world would be packed so tight there would be no room for babies.

Well, what about a commission to decide who should live and who should die? My grandfather would undoubtedly qualify for resurrection and continued life—but could I be certain the commission would recognize his special worth? Would there be cheating? Would there be mistakes? This did not appear to be a satisfactory answer either.

It was Dr. Rose, our elderly white-haired family physician, who led me to a solution; I had cherished him for his reassuring presence and care through my serious bout with scarlet fever. If Dr. Rose had been there with the right medicine, I would certainly have had my grandfather with me longer. To be a doctor was clearly the answer. For the first time my anxiety eased.

If love of my grandfather and old Dr. Rose brought me to medicine, it was my grandmother in the years that followed who showed me the strength and endurance of the elderly. This was during the Depression. We lost the farm. She and I were soon on relief, eating government-surplus foods out of cans with stigmatizing white labels. Grandmother found work in a sewing room run by the WPA, and I sold newspapers and fixed bicycles for ten cents an hour. We moved into a hotel. When I was eleven, it burned to the ground with all our possessions. We started again. And what I remember even more than the hardships of those years was my grandmother's triumphant spirit and determination. Experiencing at first hand an older person's struggle to survive, I was myself helped to survive as well.

If this book informs, illuminates, angers and guides its readers, I shall have repaid some of the debt I owe.[3]

Just because gratitude is often unexpressed does not mean that it does not exist. Gratitude does exist for senior adults and they need to receive it. Albert Schweitzer said,

When I look back upon my early days I am stirred by the thought of the number of people whom I have to thank for what they gave me or for what they were to me. At the same time I am haunted by an oppressive consciousness of the little gratitude I really showed them when I was young . . . . For all that, I think I can say with truth that I am not ungrateful. I did occasionally wake up out of that youthful thoughtlessness . . . . But down to my twentieth year, and even later still, I did not exert myself sufficiently to express the gratitude which was really in my heart. I valued too low the pleasure felt at receiving real proofs of gratitude. Often, too, shyness prevented me from expressing the gratitude I felt.

As a result of this experience with myself I refuse to think that there is so much ingratitude in the world as is commonly maintained. I have never interpreted the parable of the Ten Lepers to mean that only one was grateful. All the ten, surely, were grateful, but nine of them hurried home first . . . . One of them, however, had a disposition which made him act at once as his feelings bade him; he sought out the person who had helped him, and refreshed his soul with the assurance of his gratitude.

In the same way we ought all to make an effort to act on our first thoughts and let our unspoken gratitude find expression. Then there will be more sunshine in the world, and more power to work for what is good. But as concerns ourselves, we must all of us take care not to adopt as part of a theory of life all people's bitter sayings about the ingratitude of the world. A great deal of water is flowing underground which never comes up as a spring. In that thought we may find comfort. But we ourselves must try to be the water which does find its way up; we must become a spring at which men can quench their thirst for gratitude.[4]

Thus, this book or any of our attempts to assist or be assisted by senior adults may stem from a portion of responsibility which is fostered by obligation and gratitude.

## Honoring senior adults

The new frontier in aging has special significance for the Christian community because its background is filled with commandments and admonitions relative to attitudes and actions toward the elderly. Not the least of these is found in the Ten Commandments. John R. Claypool has noted:

There is, then, a wisdom of sequence about the Ten Commandments. This is evident not only in the context of the first four commandments, but in the fifth as well, for any discussion of human relationships must begin with the bond between parent and child. This is the first interpersonal reality that we encounter in life, and every expert from the writer of Exodus to Sigmund Freud points to its crucial significance. As goes the quality of this relation, so tends to go all the relationships of life. Therefore, we need to consider with great care the fifth of the ancient commandments: "Honor your father and your mother, that your days may be long in the land which the Lord your God gives you."[5]

The implications of this great commandment for all are obvious. Many have considered this commandment to be directed toward children; however, it was commanded of median-age adults concerning their aging parents. The true test of a civilization, a nation, a church, or a family is the esteem given to senior adults, who are, with limited exceptions, our parents.

Frank Stagg, professor emeritus of the Southern Baptist Theological Seminary, has noted the different perspectives on age which appear in Scripture, especially in the Old Testament. He maintained that "the prevailing thought is favorable to age, expecting of it understanding and wisdom, and demanding respect for it. Age is more esteemed than disparaged."[6] He further established the responsibility for respect and honor for age by referring to explicit commands found in the New Testament and the "strong accent upon age in the piety out of which John the Baptist and Jesus came (Luke 1—2)."[7]

The patriarchal Old Testament is a confirmation of honor for age. Stagg states that this perspective is so dominant "that it requires no prooftexting."[8]

*A social problem*

A sense of responsibility for senior adults, because they are a social problem, is a rather negative view. However, such a view is presented in *Why Survive?* by Robert N. Butler. Although justification exists that the book is overbalanced to the negative side, Butler uncovers the ageism that contributes to the social problem aspects of growing old. Again, others would argue that greatness may come out of adversity. Common sense teaches that barriers and negative attitudes may completely thwart those of less strength, who in a particular moment are most vulnerable. Robert Merton has suggested that "when a system of cultural value extols, virtually above all else, certain common success goals for the population at large while the social structures vigorously restricts or completely closes access to approved modes of reaching these goals for a considerable part of the population, deviant behavior ensues on a large scale."[9]

Poverty, withdrawnness, substandard housing, mental disorders, suicide, and numerous other needs of a large segment of senior adults would constitute a social problem if the following definition is accepted. "A social problem exists when a significant number of people, or a number of significant people, perceive an undesirable difference between social ideals and social realities, and believe that this difference can be eliminated by collective action."[10]

Aging, then, may be described by a large segment of our population as a social problem when: (1) it is seen as biological deterioration; (2) degradation of old age exists at a time when the number of elderly people is increasing; (3) viewed in relation to the world population explosion; (4) the plight of the aged is viewed in relation to goals for them; (5) the needs of aging are examined in light of the social norms and deviations that exist.

The influence of senior adults in regard to health care, transportation, institutional care, social security, and in countless other areas indicates a measure of what may well be called a social problem that affects each family, community/church, and the nation. A sense of responsibility is mandatory.

### Our greatest untapped resource

No experimental studies are available to substantiate the belief that senior adults are America's greatest untapped resource—only experience. The refined and growing number of longitudinal studies of senior adults, discussed later in this book, indicate that age may be an extremely productive time and one in which resides a virtual storehouse of knowledge and wisdom.

Should a sense of responsibility exist for the unshelving and uncrating of millions of years of human experience? Would not a recognition of the desperate need for and requisition of her virtues and resources meet her needs of esteem, purpose, and life sustenance?

### Prudential wisdom

As implied in the discussion of aging as a social problem, prudential wisdom quickly rises to the surface when each individual is reminded of his own senior years.

Scriptural injunctions about the image of God, obligation and gratitude, honor, and care relative to the aged are not just random directives given to force men to be obedient. They provide opportunities for man to reach fulfillment through responsibility, an element of love, as it is directed toward a most worthy object. Not only does man grow and become healed through such expressions, but there exists a realistic self-protection in meeting the needs of our elders. Joy Davidman, author of *Smoke on the Mountain,* has given us a story that is to the point in this matter of doing for others as you would have them do for you:

Once upon a time there was a little old man. His eyes blinked and his hands trembled. When he ate he clattered the silverware distressingly, missed his mouth with the spoon as often as not and dribbled a bit of his food on the table-cloth. Now he lived with his married son, having nowhere else to live, and his son's wife was a modern young woman who knew that in-laws should not be tolerated in a woman's home.

"I can't have this," she exclaimed. "It interferes with a woman's right to happiness."

So she and her husband took the little old man gently but firmly by the arm and led him to the corner of the kitchen. There they sat him on a stool and gave him his food, what there was of it, in an earthenware bowl. From then on he always ate in the corner, blinking at the table with wistful eyes.

One day his hands trembled rather more than usual, and the earthenware bowl fell and broke.

"If you are a pig," said the daughter-in-law, "you must eat out of a trough." So they made him a little wooden trough and he got his meals in that way.

These people had a four-year-old son of whom they were very fond. One suppertime the young man noticed his boy playing intently with some bits of wood and asked what he was doing.

"I'm making a trough," he said, smiling up for approval, "to feed you and mamma out of when I get big."

The man and his wife looked at each other for a while and didn't say anything. Then they cried a little. Then they went to the corner and took the little old man by the arm and led him back to the table. They sat him in a comfortable chair and gave him his food on a plate, and from then on nobody ever scolded when he clattered or spilled or broke things.[11]

Each takes his turn at aging however brief or lengthy his journey. Proper regard for one's elders whether through a sense of responsibility guided by admonition or prudential wisdom should help to enhance the value of aging and should serve the helper as well.

## A Christian psychology of aging?

The question may be raised about the attempt to write a Christian psychology of aging. Often, it has been asked in relation to different disciplines, that is, why a Christian philosophy? Others may ask in all seriousness, "Why not a Christian theory of the development of the liver?" There are those who are frightened when all natural processes are seen as alien to Christ. And the truth is, some do believe that the growth of a tree, the liver, and mental functions are nonspiritual and are separate from God. To some, the labeling of a psychology of aging as Christian is unnecessary since God set in motion the psychological aspects of man. How would calling them Christian make any difference? However, calling things Christian when they are not consistent with the truth of Christ does make a difference. Assuming that psychology in general is Christian is an error in thinking. Large differences exist between gestalt psychology, behavioristic psychology, existential psychology, and psychoanalytical psychology. Also, differences in the context and methodology of psychology exist when clinical, experimental, therapeutic, educational, and comparative psychology are practiced.

Just a casual glance at these different psychologies and their practice in different contexts, with a variety of methodologies, certainly leaves room for a psychology that is consistent with the revealed truth of Christ.

This means that the data and theoretical issues found in the various psychological views of aging will be carefully related to Christian views. Many of the observations will be derived from the latest psychological texts on aging, but always from a Christian perspective. Hopefully, a Christian psychology of senior adults will be the result.

James Hillman, director of studies at the C. G. Jung Institute in Zurich, said, "Where there is a connection to the soul, there is psychology; where not, what is taking place is better called statistics, physical anthropology, cultural journalism, or animal breeding."[12] Intense attention is given to those psychological areas which have unique implications for an understanding from a Christian perspective. Psychological needs, adjustments (shocks), development, disorders, and implications are among those which will receive this attention.

Jesus experienced earthly life as a psychological being. He was tempted in all points, suffered hunger, thirst, and experienced needs and crises of life as all men do. He had needs, adapted and adjusted, developed, wept, suffered, rejoiced, and experienced the weight of our burdens.

NOTES

[1]Wayne E. Oates, *Christ and Selfhood* (New York: Association Press, 1961), p. 147.

[2]John R. Claypool, *Claiming Your Place and Power* (Fort Worth: Broadway Baptist Church), vol. 15, #49 (September 5, 1976), 1-2.

[3]Robert N. Butler, *Why Survive?* (New York: Harper & Row, 1975), pp. ix-x.

[4]Albert Schweitzer, "Say Thank You," in *A Diary of Readings*, ed. John Baillie (New York: Charles Scribner's Sons, 1955), p. 45.

[5]John R. Claypool, "Honoring One's Parents," *Home Life*, May 1967, p. 30.

[6]Frank Stagg, "Beauty and Power of Aging" (address presented at the Southern Baptist Conference on Aging, Nashville, Tennessee, 1974), p. 11.

[7]Ibid., p. 2.

[8]Ibid.

[9]Robert K. Merton, *Social Theory and Social Structure*, rev. ed. (New York: Free Press, 1957), p. 146.

[10]Michael McKee and Ian Robertson, *Social Problems* (New York: Random House, Inc., 1975), p. 4.

[11]Joy Davidman, *Smoke on the Mountain* (Philadelphia: Westminster Press, 1953), pp. 60-61.

[12]James Hillman, *Re-Visioning Psychology* (New York: Harper & Row, Publishers, 1975), p. xii.

# 2

# Figures Don't Lie: Demographics and Other Interesting Statistics

Figures bear out the fact that America has experienced a phenomenal growth of older Americans. They also speak volumes as to their life situations so as to be relevant for generalizations for a senior-adult psychology. *Demographics,* the science of population dynamics, is considered a macro-level science, a broad overview level such as the description of what is happening to older adults in society as a whole. Psychology is at the micro-level where the focus is on the individual.[1] However, psychology is a vital discipline in *gerontology,* the science of aging, which is informed and has questions raised through the presentation of statistics.

Educational statistics and the changes that may occur as to the intelligence of senior adults may be vitally related. The incidence of dependency or living alone need to be considered when emotional problems of senior adults are studied. This section on demography presents a macro-level observation of senior adults in the areas of life expectancy trends, ratio to total population, sex ratios, comparison to other countries, ethnic comparisons, health statistics, retirement statistics, income status, location, and marital and family status. These are related to adjustment, development, and other areas of psychological functioning.

*Life expectancy trends*

In 100 B.C. the average life expectancy was only 18 years. By the year 2000 it is expected to be 73.9 years. Thus, life expectancy increased 55.9 percent in 3,000 years. It will have increased from 47.3 years of life expectancy in 1900 to 73.9 years of life expectancy in 2000, an increase of 26.6 years in 100 years. This is approximately half of the total life expectancy increase for 3,000 years. This dramatic increase already seen and predicted for the remaining two decades of this century must be seen in relation to the infant mortality rate. A more accurate assessment of increased life expectancy may be made from an analysis of the 65+ population. This group has made a gain of only three years between 1900 and 1970. Those 65+ in 1900 lived an average of 11.9 years longer while those 65+ in 1970 may expect to live an average of 15.2 years longer.

Ruth Weg, associate professor of biology/gerontology of the Leonard Davis School of Gerontology, has prepared an up-to-date summary of statistics for the Ethel Percy Andrus Center. She stressed that the dramatic increase in life expectancy does not mean that older people are living much longer. More people are reaching old age. The significant life expectancy increase has occurred in infancy and childhood.[2] In summary, life expectancy for the total population as of 1970 is 70.9 years. The life expectancy for the 65+ population as of 1970 is 80.2 years of age. See Table 1 for a study of life expectancy trends.

**TABLE 1**

**Average Life Expectancy in the United States at Birth and at Age 65 from 1900-1970**

| Age | 1900 | 1939 | 1949 | 1955 | 1959 | 1970 |
|-----|------|------|------|------|------|------|
| At Birth | 47.3 | 63.7 | 68.0 | 69.6 | 69.9 | 70.9 |
| At Age 65 | 11.9 | 12.8 | 12.8 | 14.2 | 14.4 | 15.2 |

Source: United States Public Health Service National Center for Health Statistics. *Vital Statistics of the United States: 1970,* vol. 2 + *Mortality,* Part A (Washington, D.C.: U.S. Government Printing Office), Tables 5-1 and 5-5, 1974.[3]

## Ratio to total U.S. population

Each day approximately 5,000 Americans reach 65 years of age. During that same day approximately 3,600 Americans who are 65+ die. A net of 400,000 senior adults join our population ranks each year, the result of a 1,400 per day differential. As of 1976 the total U.S. population was 215.3 million with senior adults who are 65+ accounting for 23 million or 10.5 percent of the total. This new phenomenon is no accident because 1.4 million people reach 65 every 50 weeks.[4]

In 1870 there were 1.2 million senior adults who were 65+ and comprised 3 percent of the total U.S. population. Since 1900 they have grown much faster than the rest of the population with the 75+ group now numbering 8 million. As of mid 1975, 62 percent of all senior adults 65+ were under 75; 50 percent were under 73; and 36 percent were under 70.[5]

Projections are that by 1980 senior adults will number 24.5 million, 28.9 million by 1990, and 30.6 million or 12.5 percent of the expected population by the year 2000. There will be a 60 percent increase of the 75+ population which will boost them to 44 percent of the 65+ population. Thus, older senior adults are slowly moving to a majority position among older Americans. Today there are more than 30 million people 60 and over.[6] Population figures as of July 1, 1976, showing age breakouts for senior adults are as follows:

| | |
|---|---|
| 65-69 | 8,281,000 |
| 70-74 | 5,913,000 |
| 75-79 | 4,051,000 |
| 80-85 | 2,724,000 |
| 85+ | 1,966,000 |
| | 22,935,000[7] |

## Sex ratios

The sex ratio is usually determined by comparing the number of males per 100 females in a population group.[8] The difference as to life expectancy between the sexes and other statistics indicate a need for understanding senior adults. The female, physiologically, is not superior to the male protoplasm for various reasons—and these are more than likely psychological—women outlive men in chronological age. Even though more male than female babies are born, 106 to 100, senior adult women outnumber men. "Male death rates are higher beginning at birth . . . so that by age 20 and thereafter, women increasingly outnumber men. The ratio of numbers of women in all ages reflects this, but it becomes more dramatic with increasing age, and with time from 1950-1970."[9]

Some interesting comparisons of senior adults include:

1. In mid 1970 women numbered 11.6 million while men numbered 8.4 million.

2. In mid 1973 women numbered 12.5 million while men numbered 8.8 million.

3. In mid 1975 women outnumbered men 13.2 million to 9.1 million.

4. Females report a higher number of visits by physicians than do males (1971).[10]

5. In 1964, 143.7 males and 20.3 females per 100,000 population who were 65+ committed suicide.

More detailed comparisons will be made in other specific areas of demographics. The sex ratio is expressed in tabular form for all ages (Table 2). Widowers are outnumbered by widows four to one. The custom of most women, young and old, of marrying older men has con-

**TABLE 2**

**Number of Women Compared to 100 Males in Particular Age Groupings for Selected Years[11]**

| Age Group | 1950 | 1960 | 1970 | Mid 1976 | Projection for 2000 |
|---|---|---|---|---|---|
| All ages | 101.3 | 103.0 | 105.5 | | |
| Under 45 | 100.6 | 100.5 | 100.5 | | |
| 45-64 | 99.8 | 104.5 | 109.1 | | |
| 65+ | 111.5 | 120.7 | 138.5 | 144 | 154 |
| 65-74 | 107.5 | 114.9 | 128.8 | 130 | 130 little change |
| 75+ | 120.9 | 133.1 | 156.2 | 171 | 191 |
| 85+ | | | 200+ | 200+ | |

tributed to the increasing number of widows. More than 50 percent of 65+ women are widows.[12]

## Comparison to other countries

Paul Tournier, Swiss physician, psychologist, and author, has noted that "in the West at the present time approximately one person in six is over sixty years old, and this proportion is constantly increasing. Sweden holds the record for the longest average life-span."[13] Tournier spared his reader the statistical details, and I have not done so because numbers and psychology are not good bedfellows. A comparison of several demographic statistics of the United States with other parts of the world should provide some clues of psychological, sociological, and physiological significance for understanding senior adults.

A comparison of the life expectancy at birth of males and females and percentage of the total population of five countries in five continents are shown in Table 3.

Other countries in which longer life expectancy at birth and percentage of the total population parallels are equal or greater than the United States are Japan, Canada, Austria, Denmark, France, Hungary,

**TABLE 3**

**Life Expectancy**

| Country | Year | Life Expectancy at Birth | | 65+ Percent of Total Population |
|---------|------|------|--------|---------|
| | | Male | Female | |
| United States | 1970 | 67 | 75 | 9.9 |
| Argentina | 1972 | 64.1 | 70.2 | 7.5 |
| U.S.S.R. | 1970 | 65 | 74 | 11.8 |
| Sweden | 1970 | 71.7 | 76.5 | 13.1 |
| Kenya | 1969 | 46.9 | 51.2 | 3.6 |

Source: United Nations. *Demographic Yearbook: 1972* (New York: United Nations, 1973), Tables 3 and 6.[14]

Netherlands, and the United Kingdom. All European countries have a larger ratio of senior adults to the total population than is found in the United States (early 1970's).[15] The West has a much higher ratio of senior adults to the total population than is found in the East.

Three basic processes are important in understanding demographics and contribute to an understanding of some of the different ratios of the countries mentioned above. These are fertility, or better known as the birthrate, mortality (death rate), and immigration.[16] One factor, mortality, is obviously the most important factor in the short life expectancy and ratio to the total population of many of the eastern countries. Health care, and a significant ethical and psychological concept—the valuing of life—may be construed to be important in considering the differences that exist in various countries.

*Racial population ratios*

An understanding of demographics as they relate to racial ratios may prove to be helpful. A brief summary of various statistics compiled by Ruth Weg are provided in the following outline:

1. As of July 1973 all races 65+ comprised 10.1 percent of the total population of 210,404,000 (65+ —21,329,000).

2. The white 65+ population was 19,458,000 and the black 65+ population was 1,684,000 (white, 9.2 percent; black, less than 0.9 percent of total population).

**TABLE 4**

**Size of Ethnic Groups[17]**

| Ethnic Group | Population | Percentage of Senior Adults to Total Population |
|---|---|---|
| Chinese | 435,062 | 6.22 |
| Japanese | 591,290 | 8.02 |
| Filipino | 343,060 | 6.31 |
| Samoan | 35,000 | NA |
| Mexican American | 5,023,000 | 8.44 |
| American Indian | 792,730 | 5.74 |
| American Black | 22,580,289 | 7.03 |

3. As of 1970 the populations of various ethnic groups (all ages) were as shown in Table 4.

4. Foreign born senior adults comprise 15 percent of the 65+ population.[18]

5. "A 75-year-old black woman could expect to outlive a white man of the same age by 3.2 years, a black man by 2.1 years, and a white woman by 0.9 years."[19]

6. Whites 65+ comprised 10.3 percent of all whites in the U.S. while elderly blacks were 7 percent of the total black population. A higher infant death rate for blacks and a present higher fertility rate may account for this difference.[20]

Racial ratios are presented in other areas of demographics in this section. They will be presented in relation to education, health, income, and so forth.

*Education*

What are the formal education levels of our elderly population? This question is related to various psychological functions such as I.Q., learning, and speed of response. A few summary statements may suffice as opposed to elaborate tables.

1. The elderly have not completed as many years of formal education as have younger adults. However, the present young adults who are better educated will eventually be tomorrow's senior adults. By 1990 approximately 50 percent of the senior adult population will be high school graduates.

2. As of 1970, 4.2 percent of persons 65+ had had no formal schooling.[21] Ruth Weg stated that in 1972 more than two million of the 65+ population was "functionally illiterate."[22] Thus, approximately 10 percent are seriously impaired educationally. Such a statistic may be psychologically more important but may be related to problems of health, income, and so forth.

3. As of 1974, senior adults averaged four years less of formal schooling than the 25-64 age group. This fact may be due to the unavailability of schools and lack of emphasis on formal education, especially for the 15 percent who were foreign born.[23]

4. In 1974, women had more formal education than men with men having two extremes, little education and more college than women.

5. In 1970, the median years of education for the over 65 group was 8.7. This figure reflected an increase of a half year in the 1960's. An increase of two years is projected for the 1980's.

6. Urban senior adults have more formal education than rural aged (1974).

7. Seven percent of older people had graduated from college by 1974.[24]

Improvement of educational levels will continue well beyond 1990 as our educated adolescents of the 1960's and 1970's become the senior adults of the twenty-first century. "The 2010-2020 'gerontology boom' will be a well-educated group of people."[25] In Table 5 future education levels of the 65+ age group are projected.

*Residential distribution*

In 1970 the 65+ group, who lived in urban areas, numbered 14.6 million, or 73 percent. Over one half of these resided in heavily urbanized areas. This disproportionate concentration of senior adults in central cities engenders legitimate concern about problems of crime, transportation, congestion, living costs, and housing.[26]

**TABLE 5**

**Projections of Future Educational Levels
of the 65+ Population in the United
States from 1975-1990[27]**

| | | Years of School Completed | | |
|---|---|---|---|---|
| Year | No school | Elementary 1-8 years | High school 1-4 years or more | College 1 year or more |
| 1975 | 0.6 | 52.0 | 33.8 | 13.6 |
| 1980 | 0.5 | 45.9 | 38.7 | 14.9 |
| 1985 | 0.4 | 39.0 | 44.4 | 16.2 |
| 1990 | 0.4 | 32.9 | 49.2 | 17.5 |

Source: Adapted from United States Bureau of the Census. *Current Population Reports,* Series P-25, No. 476, "Demographic Projections for the United States" (February, 1972), Tables 3 and 5.

Senior adults are the largest proportion of the total population of small rural towns (places of 1,000 to 2,500 total population). They achieve a 13.6 percent ratio. The elderly are a larger proportion of each area where the population is less dense with the exception of the farm areas. This residential pattern is consistent from the highly peopled urbanized areas down the scale to the small towns but not farming areas. This may be explained partially by the movement to small towns from the depressed farm areas during World War II.[28]

The largest proportion of the elderly poor live in the rural nonfarm areas, with the rural farm areas following, and the smallest proportion in urban areas.[29]

Where are senior adults according to regions? As of 1970, the most populous region was the North with over six million of the 65+ group residing there. Next, the North Central region follows with 5.7 million. The Northeast region (New England and Middle Atlantic states) is the third most populous area with nearly 5.2 million. The West is the least populous region with 3.1 million but has gained more than the North Central and Northeast regions since 1960. The South has made a much larger gain than the other three regions.[30]

In which states are the largest groups of senior adults residing? The ten states with the largest concentrations of the 65+ group are shown in Table 6.

These data reveal population migration trends that should alert the South, especially the South Atlantic states, and the West to the increasing growth potential of the 65+ group in their region. Although several Northeastern states have large concentrations of senior adults, these may continue to see a net drop in senior-adult population even though the number of elderly continues to grow.

Because several states show high rates of in- or out-migration the mobility of the 65+ group may be misunderstood. This group as a whole has the lowest mobility. The trend would indicate that the movement which is occurring is going in only two directions, South and West. Ruth Weg reports:

In March 1975, 75% of all elderly people lived in the same house they did in 1970. Of the 20% who moved, 12% remained in the same county, 4% remained

## TABLE 6

### The Population and Percentage Increase of the 65+ Group in Ten States with Largest Concentration: 1970[31]

| Rank | State | Number | Percent increase since 1960 | Percent of state total in 1970 |
|------|-------|--------|------------------------------|--------------------------------|
| 1 | New York | 1,961,000 | 16.2 | 10.8 |
| 2 | California | 1,801,000 | 30.9 | 9.0 |
| 3 | Pennsylvania | 1,272,000 | 12.7 | 10.8 |
| 4 | Illinois | 1,094,000 | 12.2 | 9.8 |
| 5 | Ohio | 998,000 | 11.2 | 9.4 |
| 6 | Texas | 992,000 | 33.1 | 8.9 |
| 7 | Florida | 989,000 | 78.9 | 14.6 |
| 8 | Michigan | 753,000 | 18.0 | 8.5 |
| 9 | New Jersey | 697,000 | 24.4 | 9.7 |
| 10 | Massachusetts | 636,000 | 11.3 | 11.2 |

Source: Adapted from United States Bureau of the Census. *Census of Population: 1970, General Population Characteristics,* (Washington, D.C.: United States Government Printing Office) Final Report, PC (1)-B1, Tables 59 and 62; *Census of Population: 1960, Characteristics of the Population, Volume 1,* Part 1 (Washington, D.C.: United States Government Printing Office) United States Summary, Tables 55 and 59.

in the same state, and 4% moved to a different state and of this 4% only 3% moved to a noncontiguous state. Migrations to Florida, Arizona, and Nevada, primarily because of climate.[32]

The assumption that the elderly population in the United States is a homogeneous group is false. A "sociocultural homogeneity" was found in certain regions but was not congruent with the traditional state or regional groupings. One research effort revealed that bordering states have elderly populations who are quite similar according to twenty sociological and economic indicators but that greater differences exist today than in 1960. This finding would indicate that an elderly population can be characterized only in terms specific to that population.[33]

## Employment

In 1900, approximately 67 percent of men 65+ were in the labor force. Statistics as of May 1975 reveal a steady decline has persisted until approximately one out of every four males was employed. An opposite trend occurred for senior adult women up until the early 1970's when their participation began to decline. This may be due in large measure to increased retirement benefits for women. Three different age groupings for men and three for women are presented in Table 7.

Approximately 75 percent of men 65+ and approximately 85 percent of women 65+ are economically inactive. This unemployment exists for many senior adults who want and need work. The recent enactment of legislation which raises the mandatory retirement age to 70 may reverse the trends depicted in Table 7.

**TABLE 7**

**Percentage of the Elderly Participating in the Labor Force by Age and Sex, 1940 through 1975[34]**

| Sex and Age Group | 1940 | 1950 | 1960 | 1970 | 1975* |
|---|---|---|---|---|---|
| Men | | | | | |
| 65 through 69 | 59.4 | 59.7 | 44 | 39.3 | 33.3 |
| 70 through 74 | 38.4 | 38.7 | 28.7 | 22.5 | 14.9 |
| 75 and over | 18.2 | 18.7 | 15.6 | 12.1 | |
| Women | | | | | |
| 65 through 69 | 9.5 | 13 | 16.5 | 17.2 | 14.6 |
| 70 through 74 | 5.1 | 6.4 | 9.6 | 9.1 | 5.2 |
| 75 and over | 2.3 | 2.6 | 4.3 | 4.7 | |

Sources: U.S. Bureau of the Census, *Employment Status and Work Experience,* Subject Report PC(2)-6A (Washington, D.C.: United States Government Printing Office, 1973), pp. 31-32; and U.S. Department of Labor, Bureau of Labor Statistics, *Employment and Earnings,* Vol. 21, No. 12 (Washington, D.C.: United States Government Printing Office, 1975), pp. 29-30.

*As of May 1975.

## Dependency ratio

Statistics about the number of senior adults who are not working are important for an understanding of the 65 + population and its relation to the younger, supportive population. The dependency ratio is particularly informative during these days when most of the 65 + population are receiving more from Social Security than they have paid into it. Thus, the dependency ratio is simply determined by dividing the increasing older group by the 18-64 age group. As the younger supportive group gets smaller and the older group gets larger the dependency ratio increases. A psychology of aging may be informed by a consideration of this factor as to the thoughts and feelings of senior adults and the supportive group in regard to the implications of the dependency ratio. Table 8 shows an alarming trend.

The dependency ratio is projected for no change from 1970 to 2000. In large part, this may be explained by the smaller number born at the turn of the century and through the depression years. Fertility and mortality were the determining processes. The World War II "baby boom" accounts for the dramatic projected change from 2000 to 2050.

**TABLE 8**

**Dependency Ratios for the 65 + Age Group
in the United States: 1930-2050[35]**

| 1930 | 1940 | 1950 | 1960 | 1970 | 2000 | 2020 | 2050 |
|------|------|------|------|------|------|------|------|
| .097 | .118 | .133 | .167 | .177 | .177 | .213 | .257 |

Sources: (1930-1940) U.S. Bureau of the Census, *U.S. Census Population: 1940.* Characteristics of the Population, Table 8, p. 26. (1950-1970) U.S. Bureau of the Census, *Statistical Abstract of the United States:* 1972, Table 37, p. 32. (2000 + based on Series E projections) Herman B. Brotman, "Projections of the Population to the Year 2000." Statistical Memo #25, Administration on Aging (June 1973), p. 3. (2020, 2050 + based on Series E and Series W, respectfully), prepared by Dr. David M. Heer, Population Research Laboratory, University of Southern California, February 1974.

*Health facts*

Psychological problems developed from one's physical condition are receiving increasing attention in medicine. Also, problems growing out of psychological problems are receiving renewed emphasis as the inter relatedness of body and mind is confirmed. Health facts may provide clues to psychological functioning and vice versa. A listing of general health statistics follows:

1. Senior adults have twice as many hospital stays and twice as long as the rest of the population.[36]

2. A study of the noninstitutionalized population of the United States showed that only 83 percent of the 65 + population reported no hospital-ization in the 1974-75 year. This would indicate that approximately 17 percent of the senior adults account for twice as many hospital stays, etc., and a much smaller percentage probably account for the majority of hospital stays.[37]

3. In 1967, 86 percent of the noninstitutionalized 65 + population had one or more chronic conditions.[38]

4. In 1972, fewer acute conditions were reported for the older age group than all other groups.[39]

5. Children under 6 and adults 45 years and above had a slightly higher number of days of restricted activity from acute conditions in 1972.[40]

6. In 1972, 43.2 percent of the 65 + group reported that they had some activity limitation due to chronic condition(s). Limitation in a major activity (for example, working, keeping house, or going to school) was reported by 97.9 percent.

7. The 65 + group reported fewer injuries than the other age group listed in the study. Groups listed are (1) under 6 years, (2) 6-16 years, (3) 17-44 years, (4) 45-64 years, and (5) 65 years and over.[41]

The psychological implications of the preceding demographic informa-tion are fairly obvious as the senior adult population is viewed as a whole. Adjustment tasks or psychological shocks as outlined in chapter 5 will rely heavily on these demographics.

## NOTES

[1]Neal E. Cutler and Robert A. Harootyan, "Demography of the Aged," in *Aging: Scientific Perspectives and Social Issues,* eds. Diana S. Woodruff and James E. Birren (New York: D. Van Nostrand Co., 1975), p. 31.

[2]Ruth B. Weg, "The Aged: Who, Where, How Well (Education, Health, Income and Marital Status)" (Los Angeles: Ethel Percy Andrus Gerontology Center, 1977; reprint ed., Athens, Ga.: Project-GIST, 1978), p. 3.

[3]Cutler and Harootyan, "Demography of the Aged," p. 32.

[4]Weg, "The Aged: Who, Where, How Well," p. 1.

[5]Ibid.

[6]Ibid., pp. 2-3.

[7]Ibid., p. 3.

[8]Cutler and Harootyan, "Demography of the Aged," p. 48.

[9]Weg, "The Aged: Who, Where, How Well," p. 3.

[10]Ibid., p. 7.

[11]Ibid., p. 4.

[12]Ibid.

[13]Paul Tournier, *Learn to Grow Old,* trans. Edwin Hudson (London: SCM Press Ltd., 1972), p. 2.

[14]Cutler and Harootyan, "Demography of the Aged," p. 48.

[15]Ibid.

[16]Ibid., pp. 37-45.

[17]Weg, "The Aged: Who, Where, How Well," pp. 17-18.

[18]Ibid.

[19]Leon Bouvier, Elinore Atlee, and Frank McVeigh, "The Elderly in America," in *Readings in Aging and Death: Contemporary Perspectives,* ed. Steven H. Zarit (New York: Harper & Row, Pub., 1977), p. 31.

[20]Ibid.

[21]Ibid., p. 33.

[22]Weg, "The Aged: Who, Where, How Well," p. 17.

[23]Ibid.

[24]Ibid.

[25]Cutler and Harootyan, "Demography of the Aged," p. 65.

[26]Ibid., p. 55.

[27]Ibid., p. 65.

[28]Ibid., p. 55.

[29]Weg, "The Aged: Who, Where, How Well," p. 5.

[30]Bouvier, Atlee, and McVeigh, "Elderly in America," p. 31.

[31]Cutler and Harootyan, "Demography of the Aged," p. 56.

[32]Weg, "The Aged: Who, Where, How Well," p. 5.

[33]Cary S. Kart and Barbara B. Manard, eds., *Aging in America: Readings in Social Gerontology* (Port Washington, N.Y.: Alfred Publishing Co., Inc., 1976), pp. 109-23.

[34]Bouvier, Atlee, and McVeigh, "Elderly in America," p. 33.

[35]Cutler and Harootyan, "Demography of the Aged," p. 48.

[36]Weg, "The Aged: Who, Where, How Well," p. 5.

[37]Ibid., p. 6.

[38]Ibid.

[39]Ibid.

[40]U.S. Public Health Service, *Current Estimates from the Health Interview Survey, United States: 1972,* Vital and Health Statistics Series 10, No. 85, DHEW Publication No. (HRA) 74-1512 (Rockville, Maryland: U.S. Public Health Service, 1973), p. 12.

[41]Ibid., p. 17.

# 3

# Psychological Functions

Usually psychological functions are thought of as being mentalistic or, at least, in some way distinctive from physical functions. A line of demarcation between the physical and biological sciences (inanimate and animate) is difficult to draw. Also, the interrelatedness of the biological to the psychological thrusts the same problem upon us. Distinguishing between mind and soul has been equally as perplexing. In reality, all functions (physiological, biological, psychological, and spiritual) are functions of a living soul. "God . . . breathed into his nostrils the breath of life; and man became a living soul."[1] However, certain functions which make man different from an animal are those which are distinctive functions of a living soul. Even though Erich Fromm would not hold to many of our Christian views he felt that modern psychology has neglected the soul of man.

Psychological functions which appear to have particular relevancy for an understanding of distinctive qualities of a living soul are conscience, will, awareness of death, and so forth. These functions will be discussed further in chapter 5 ("Adjustments and Development"). Traditional psychological functions and their relationship to aging will be investigated in this chapter. These functions are: intelligence, sensory functions, memory, learning, attitudes, and sensorimotor response. Motivation will be related to personality development in chapter 5.

## Intelligence and the Senior Adult

What is intelligence? How is it measured and what does aging have to do with this mental function? These are pertinent questions and, hopefully, helpful answers will follow in the next few pages.

*Definition of intelligence*

Intelligence can be defined simply as the ability to learn and know. Sir Francis Galton, British aristocrat, mathematician, and psychologist, was interested in the origins of genius and because of this attempted to devise means of measuring human mental capacities. He thought that the bases of intelligence were simple factors such as the ability to discriminate with the senses and to react quickly. Alfred Binet, a Frenchman, differed with Galton. Together with Theodore Simon, a psychiatrist, they constructed in 1905 the first intelligence test. Binet thought that the concept "intelligence" involved a comprehensive array of traits. He included memory, imagery, imagination, attention, suggestibility, comprehension, aesthetic appreciation, motor skills, moral ideas, and willpower as components of intelligence.

In the main, since Galton and Binet, two points of view have prevailed. One view, the theory that intelligence is composed of various independent mental capacities, is associated with the name, L. L. Thurstone. He believed that intelligence is a composite of several primary mental abilities that are entirely independent. For example, a person good in mathematics may be poor in word fluency. The other main view is associated with the name, C. Spearman. He believed that intelligence was composed of several mental abilities and a factor common to all abilities that he named "g" (for general). He contended that a person with a lot of "g" could test well in all mental abilities. Later, Thurstone moved toward this view.[2] Table 9 presents Thurstone's list of primary mental abilities in intelligence and examples of their meaning.[3]

From the brief survey presented in Table 9 the reader can understand something of the wide disagreements and criticisms that exist about the concept of intelligence. Because of this confusion a third view developed which simply suggests that "Intelligence is whatever the intelligence tests test."[4] Since predictions of success in school have been the primary use of intelligence tests, why not find out what lies behind this success rather than define intelligence.[5]

By briefly considering some of the background of conceptualizing and defining intelligence, suspicions are aroused as to the accuracy of prior and existing I.Q. tests for senior adults.

## TABLE 9

### Thurstone's Primary Mental Abilities
### and Examples of Their Meaning[6]

| Primary Ability | Explanations of How Tested |
| --- | --- |
| Verbal comprehension | Reading comprehension, understanding analogies and proverbs; vocabulary |
| Word fluency | Rhyming; working anagram problems; generating words in a given category |
| Space | Perceiving geometric relations accurately; visualizing transformations in geometric relations |
| Associative memory | Rote memory, particularly for paired associates |
| Perceptual speed | Grasping details accurately, noting quickly similarities and differences |
| General reasoning | Finding rules governing particular sets of instances, as in completing number series |

Source: From Anastasi, 1968, pp. 329-30.


## *The intelligence-quotient (I.Q.)*

We have heard for years about "I.Q." Children have been psychologically maimed and senior adults have resigned themselves to dumbness because of reports of low I.Q. scores. What is this statistic that is the hallmark of the psychometric approach and is so psychologically powerful? The formula for I.Q. is:

$$I.Q. = \frac{M.A.}{C.A.} \times 100$$

The chronological age is represented by C.A. and the mental age by M.A. A person's mental age is calculated on the basis of how well he scores on the I.Q. test as compared with a large sample of his own age group.

## Correcting early tests of senior adults

In the 1930's, 1940's, and 1950's senior adult I.Q. test scores were interpreted in comparison with younger age groups. Intelligence was said to reach its peak in young adulthood and drop thereafter. Thus, much of the earlier data reported a decline in aging and perpetuated the myth of a loss of intelligence. Paul B. Baltes and K. Warner Schaie, two research psychologists, largely dispelled this myth in "The Myth of the Twilight Years," an article printed in *Psychology Today* in 1974. Following ten years of intensive research, Baltes, Schaie, and other colleagues now promote an optimistic view of intelligence in the aged. They report, "Intelligence does not slide downhill from adulthood through old age. By many measures, it increases as time goes by."[7] This new understanding of the relation of aging to intelligence came as a result of conflicting data derived from two different types of research. Older research efforts were cross-sectional, a type of research which tested various age groupings simultaneously. A different type is longitudinal research—the testing of age groups or individuals independently over a substantial period of time. As previously stated, the earlier, cross-sectional studies provided data which was interpreted as I.Q. decline. Better tests of intelligence and longitudinal studies provided data which were not in agreement with earlier testing. The discrepancy has been almost resolved following Schaie's cross-sectional testing and longitudinal testing of a large sample of senior adults in 1956 and the retesting of them later in 1963. When the results were interpreted, by comparing one group to another group (cross-sectional style), a pattern of decline was seen for senior adults. However, when the results were analyzed longitudinally (comparing a given group's performance in 1956 with its performance in 1963), a pattern of decline was seen in only one of four measures of intelligence. In two dimensions of intelligence people over 70 years of age improved from the first testing to the second.[8]

## A generation gap

The existence of a generation gap is one main factor in the inaccurate assessment of declining I.Q. in senior adults. The fact that one age group is different from another age group is obvious. This fact does not mean that people of different ages are incompatible and cannot live in harmony. It does mean that people have different values, educational attainments, histories, and so forth. Because of these facts it is not reasonable to assume that senior adults have declined intellectually when their I.Q.'s are found to be lower than that found in a younger group. People who are fifty years of age if tested would have different scores from fifty-year-olds tested ten years from now. The difference would not be due to chronological age but to generational differences. Thus, the most important factor in intellectual differences between various age groupings is the year of birth. These generational differences are speculated to be the result of the educational content, teaching methodology, and length of formal education.[9]

The informal education distinctive of each generation and locality would contribute to generational differences. Limited educational facilities, training levels of teachers, the value of education, the practicability of much educational content, and encouragement from parents or society, are other factors that contribute to generational differences in intelligence.[10]

Wide differences exist within a single generation of senior adults. A seventy-year-old American Negro, American Indian, or American Caucasian may possess an abundance of wisdom and information pertinent to his respective culture. A test could possibly be devised to measure a generally shared area of knowledge among them. However, such a test would appear to be extremely limited in measuring abilities which are largely determined by culture. These intragenerational differences were not properly accounted for in previous cross-sectional or longitudinal tests.

The attitudes of a generation as to willingness to volunteer responses and as to sophistication in test-taking are crucial factors in generational differences. Add to this the inability to construct a suitable test for several or all generations and now we can see a generation gap, especially in cross-sectional testing.[11]

### Distance from death

Studies of the intelligence of senior adults may be skewed substantially by the presence in the sample of a number who are approaching death. A small number of senior adults who experience a drastic drop in I.Q. may be close to death. This drop is called "terminal drop" by Klaus and Ruth Riegel in "Life, or Death and I.Q." In 1956, the Riegels tested 380 German men and women, 55-75 years of age. Five years later they retested 202 of the original 380. A number refused. The researchers found that several of the first testing group had died during the intervening five years. Upon checking the scores of those deceased, the Riegels found the scores were lower than the others. Five years later in 1966 a follow-up study was made. Again, those who died had scored lower than the others, and, many of those who refused to be tested were more likely to have died than the others. The Riegels theorized that perhaps their refusal to take the tests indicated an awareness of their condition.[12]

Two other studies conducted by M. A. Liberman in 1965 and 1966 confirm the idea of systematic changes in cognitive functioning as the senior adults approached death. Those who were tested in the 1965 study showed no cognitive function change if they lived two years past the study. Changes were noted in those who died six to nine months after the study. Thus, the effects of approaching death disturb cognitive functioning within a nine-month period before death.[13] The 1965 and 1966 studies seemed to indicate that death-near (DN) subjects experienced a total system decline.[14] D. B. Bromley reported a slight larger time-frame for death-near subjects. He said " . . . age-changes in intellectual performance and in EEG appear to become more marked in the two or three years preceding the death of the elderly person."[15]

*Biased I.Q. tests*

I.Q. tests have been prepared in general for children and youth. The main purpose of these instruments was to predict success in formal schooling. Thus, they are prepared in a particular generation by test constructors of another generation for children and youth who represent select generations. The content of the tests is in large measure prepared with a particular period of the individual's history in mind. The language, of necessity, is representative of a particular period of culture.

The abilities measured may vary according to particular I.Q. tests but usually these abilities are those characteristic of or important to youth. The concept of intelligence may not have been broadened sufficiently to incorporate abilities distinctive of senior adults. Or, we do not know the distinctive intellectual abilities of senior adults. Much research needs to be done at this point.

The format and speed requirements of most tests suggest an age-bias. Many senior adults are somewhat shackled by poor eyesight, bifocals, arthritis, and other problems. Some of these difficulties affect performance, if print is small and dexterity required. What is measured is the faculty of seeing, a largely psychological function. However, seeing is not generally conceptualized as a dimension of intelligence. Other physiological factors, such as fatigue and pain which are heightened by the length and intensity of tests, may represent an age-bias when the health problems of senior adults are not allowed for in the tests.

## A new description of intelligence

Galton's early description of intelligence was limited to the senses and reaction time. Binet's conceptualization was much more elaborate. L. L. Thurstone's and C. Spearman's conceptualizations appeared to be much more mentalistic and less elaborate than Binet's. Thurstone's primary mental abilities are found in Table 9. However, a four-dimensional conceptualization of intelligence was theorized by K. Warner Schaie in the late 1950's and early 1960's. Schaie is now associate director for research and professor of psychology at the Andrus Gerontology Center. Through a research study using both the cross-sectional and longitudinal types he tested five hundred subjects from 21 to 70 years of age. He gave the same tests to 301 of the subjects seven years later. He reported,

The tests we used yielded 13 separate measures of cognitive functioning. Using factor-analysis methods, we found that the scores reflected four general, fairly independent dimensions of intelligence: 1) *Crystallized intelligence* encompasses the sorts of skills one acquires through education and aculteration, such as verbal comprehension, numerical skills, and deductive reasoning. To a large degree, it reflects the extent to which one has accumulated the collective intelligence of one's own culture. It is the dimension tapped by most traditional I.Q. tests (see "Are I.Q. Tests Intelligent?" by Raymond Cattell, PT, March 1968). 2) *Cognitive flexibility* measures the ability to shift from one way of thinking to another, within the context of familiar intellectual operations, as when one must provide either an antonym or synonym to a word, depending on whether the word appears in capital or lower-case letters. 3) *Visuo-motor flexibility* measures a similar, but independent skill, the one involved in shifting from familiar to unfamiliar patterns in tasks requiring coordination between visual and motor abilities, e.g., when one must copy words but interchange capitals with lower-case letters. 4) Finally, *visualization* measures the ability to organize and process visual materials, and involves tasks such as finding a simple figure contained in a complex one or identifying a picture that is complete.[16]

## Summary

Many of the faults of earlier investigations of the intelligence of senior adults have been eliminated. Tests are administered to the same group or same individuals over many years and are designed to be more appropriate for the elderly, for example, test problems are based on using the telephone book. New conceptualizations of intelligence which include mental abilities that have come to be respected as wisdom, demonstrate gains rather than decline. A reduction in the speed of response is indicated but is not significant when all of the dimensions of intelligence are considered. Senior adults who are physically healthy do not lose their judgment, ability to abstract, or knowledge. The store of information may increase as well as inductive reasoning and vocabulary may increase until very near the end of life.

## Sensory Functions and the Senior Adult

One may wonder why the senses are almost always included in studies of psychological functions. Seeing, hearing, touching, smelling, tasting, and other special senses are open for inspection and evaluation by everyone whether they are psychologists or not. They appear to be more physiological than psychological. In fact, John Watson, the father of American behaviorism, wanted to do away with everything mentalistic. He theorized that man was nothing more than a stimulus response machine, and he viewed his behavior as the result of conditioned glandular and muscular responses in the body. If this view prevailed, then sensory functions would not be included in psychological studies.

Too much evidence is available to prevent us from too narrow a view of how man receives the world. To hold to an overbalanced physiological view as to these bridges between man and his world as mechanistic, wide-open to all stimuli and not selective or subject to psychological predispositions.

At this moment, I am concerned about a twelve-year-old poodle, Tiger, who appears to have almost suddenly lost much of his hearing ability. (Mind you, I am much more concerned about the hearing losses of many of our senior adults.) But I can try all kinds of tricks on him to test his hearing without considering myself disrespectful. This poodle is in love with my wife, and because of a slight jealousy, I suspect that he has just about tuned me out. Well, if that is true, it is psychological! It is surprising when I imitate her and call him how much better he responds. Many women will attest that no formal experimental studies are needed to prove that men hear only what they want to hear. This is true for both sexes.

At this very moment stimuli are impinging on me from all directions—lights, the touch of my pen, the cool air from the air conditioner, the old heater (ugly thing) viewed to my right; tastes, smells, and literally thousands of other stimuli could be isolated in a given moment. Usually, you do not sort them out. Just a few are given attention. Much assails us below the level of consciousness. These have made some impact, however limited it may be, but in most instances we do not respond to each consciously. Thus, because of interests, pressures, attitudes, and many factors other than physiological factors, certain sensory impressions are registered consciously. Of course, they are largely made possible by the physical structures of the sensorium. The wholistic view of man clearly explicates the interrelatedness of the physical, psychological, and spiritual. This view has been espoused by numerous scholars of the Christian doctrine of man.

Another strong indication of the place of psychology in sensory functions is seen in severe mental disorders. Hallucinations, usually the telltale signs of psychosis, are defined as false sensory impressions.

These often provide significant clues for understanding a person psychologically and spiritually. In schizophrenia, a severe mental disorder, a primary symptom is looseness of association. This symptom may be best understood as a problem of subordinating many ideas and allowing only pertinent and closely related ideas to occupy one's attention. Thus, the inability to subordinate unrelated ideas has a companion problem, the inability to subordinate much of the stimuli bombarding the senses. This accounts for the withdrawal and confusion that is so common in this illness. To see, hear, feel, touch, and taste our environment almost simultaneously is overwhelming.

Experimental studies of the senses have multiplied over the years. All the evidence points to losses in sensory acuity for senior adults in general. Many questions are unanswered as to whether the decline is mainly an inevitable deterioration that flows from built-in obsolescence or from exogenous factors (negative, destructive factors in the environment). Thus, what may be described as *decline equals aging* is likely *decline is the product of a destructive environment.*

In general, losses do occur. They may be the result of exogenous factors, built-in factors, or the result of psychological dynamics. Without doubt, there are many psychological consequences as a result of the losses. The senior adult receives less sensory information; the information he does receive tends to be ambiguous. Thus, older persons are more cautious about environmental messages. This uncertainty about the environment may precipitate a distrust of oneself and in particular, persons in their social orbit. Soft inuendos in conversation, vocal sounds directed away from the older person, noises outside the house and on the street at night, signs, flowers, and flavorful meals are a few of the sensory stimuli that become difficult to sense properly. The rich, beautiful, and subtle physical world gradually shrinks.[17] Yet, such losses may allow more room for beautiful spiritual messages that may pour forth from a lifetime of sensing God's beautiful world. Many senior adults have enough sensory experiences to keep them busy enjoying them for eternity. In fact, a few sensory experiences may allow for more savoring of each one.

*Vision*

Experimental studies of senior adults indicate a lack of flexibility in the lens. Also, "the pupil size of the eye tends to diminish with age, thus reducing the amount of light reaching the retina."[18] Many older adult persons develop a cataract condition that causes a glare because of the scattering effect of this condition. Most senior adults, without cataracts, are sensitive to glare. This fact alerts us to the dangers of glare in night driving and the blinding that occurs when light fixtures are placed at eye level. Lighting that is strong, indirect, and diffused is much better for most senior adults. Table and floor lamps and unshielded overhead lights are dangerous.

Because of the reduced input of light due to smaller pupil size, illumination should be doubled for the sixty-year-old as compared to a youth of twenty. At eighty the light needs to be tripled. Also, because of lens rigidity, the ability to accommodate to changes in light is slower. Moving from intense light to dark and vice versa may cause many accidents unless one is aware of this change. Also, a change in color vision develops because of a yellowing of the lens.

The lens become slightly yellow and filters out violet, blue, and green colors at the dark end of the spectrum. For older people to get the same satisfaction from colors in their environment, there must be more yellow, orange, and red around. Age brings a tendency to farsightedness, and visual acuity tends to decline, although these two trends vary greatly from person to person.[19]

*Hearing*

One of the most troublesome sensory losses to senior adults is the loss of hearing. Anthropological studies of African tribes have caused serious questions to be raised about age being the culprit. The studies found almost no hearing loss in some of the uncivilized tribes. As is true in so many instances of human deterioration, a harsh environment may be the primary cause. Some would answer, "Well, isn't that what aging is, the wear and tear of living in a world that beats upon the individual?" No, that is not what aging is! Men dying of dreaded diseases; others crippled from accidents, pollution, and thousands of other destructive forces that can or should be prevented must not be called "aging." Because of the passage of time amid a not-too-gentle environment, all kinds of deterioration are found in those who are chronologically older. Unfortunately, they are equated with aging.

Senior adults, in general, experience a decline in their ability to hear high-pitched sounds and soft sounds. For some unknown reason, men show this loss, beginning at approximately age fifty-five, more than do women. Airline pilots have shown a loss of hearing in the ear that was closest to the airplane motors. The noise-polluted working conditions of many men may be the chief cause of their earlier hearing loss.

An article by Joseph J. Rizzo, director of the Better Hearing Institute, in *Seventeen* magazine focused on how the present-day noise level affects many young people. He said that excessive noise had made hearing loss the nation's number one disability. More than five million Americans have permanent hearing disorders, and they are under eighteen. The number is rapidly climbing. He indicated that noise can precipitate headaches, nausea, tension, and anxiety. Also, researchers are linking prolonged noise with mental disorders, ulcers, indigestion, heart disease, and impaired learning ability. Noise robs the individual of concentration while awake. During sleep, he is robbed of rest by being pushed out of the dream state or prevented from entering it. Heart rate, blood pressure, and other bodily functions are affected by prolonged periods of noise. An alarming fact is that hearing loss is speeding up. What was the consequence of many years of buffeting the individual now takes approximately one third as long.

The Noise Study Laboratory of the University of Tennessee surveyed over four thousand freshmen. Sixty percent suffered from some hearing impairment. Rizzo offered some practical helps in recognizing signs of beginning hearing loss. They are

. . . Consistent inability to hear words or phrases
. . . Inability to understand conversation in a group
. . . The ability to comprehend better when facing a speaker
. . . Discharge from the ear, pain, or irritation
. . . Dizziness, unsteadiness or head noises.[20]

*Taste and smell*

Although most studies have indicated a decrease in taste sensitivity with age, the findings are not consistent. Some studies have not verified this decrease. There appears to be a particular dislike among senior adults for that which tastes bitter. However, this may be just a matter of preference rather than heightened sensitivity. No firm conclusions can be drawn at this time about changes in the ability of senior adults as to taste.[21] Some studies have reported that by sixty years of age 50 percent of the taste buds are lost and by seventy only one sixth of the taste buds remain. In spite of these losses major changes do not occur until after age seventy.

Also, no strong conclusions can be drawn about the relation of the sense of smell to aging. Odor sensitivity does appear to be more stable and durable in the senior adult than is taste. Decreases in taste or smell sensitivity may have been the result of disease, sex differences, and smoking. Preferences for certain odors were found to change with age, but this occurred rather early in life and has been associated with maturation and learning rather than aging.[22]

*Somesthesis* (touch, pain, temperature, vibration, muscle, and joint senses)

Somesthesis is a concept that includes those sensations that result from stimulation of the skin, viscera (heart, stomach, liver, kidneys, and intestines), muscle, and joint senses. Thus, touch, pain, temperature, vibration, and position of limbs and joints are a part of somesthesis.[23] Of course, the question is, "How does advancing age affect the individual's response to the sensations just mentioned?"

Prior to 1970 little research had been done on touch sensitivity, but there was some suggestion that a decline occurs in the senior years.[24] Dan R. Kenshalo, Florida State University, implies from his studies that changes in somesthetic sensitivity (touch, pain, and so on) are the consequences of growing older. However, he insists on tentative conclusions at this point. He wrote:

It should be borne in mind, however, that these (changes) may not be due directly and exclusively to aging, per se, but may also result from the increased probability, with added years of life, of the occurrence of injury or pathological conditions that affect the skin, the receptors, or the nervous system.[25]

In the general population, regardless of cause, a decline in sensitivity to touch, temperature, vibration, pain, muscle, and joint sensations is experienced. We need to understand the importance of this information in being alerted to disease (pain), falling (muscle, joint, vibration, and touch sensations), and comfort (temperature). A decline, however slight, must be understood in order to provide adequate safeguards.

## Learning and Senior Adults

One of the most widely held myths, both in and out of formal educational circles, is the myth that older adults are severely handicapped in their ability to learn. This destructive myth is predicated on the belief that learning ability peaks in young adulthood then declines constantly due to the inherent effects of the aging process. The myth is perpetuated in such statements as: "All older people become senile." "You can't tell them anything." "You can't teach an old dog new tricks." "Old people are unflexible, they will not change." "Old people become just like little children." "Special educational methods are necessary to deal with the unique problems of older Americans."

Dr. Roger DeCrow, director of the Older Americans Project states:

One of the strangest delusions in history is the still prevalent myth, that older people cannot learn or that they typically suffer serious decline in mental abilities.

Common sense observation should dispel this notion for hundreds of thousands of older adults are learning in the programs reported in our survey and millions have learned every imaginable subject in adult education programs over the years and decades.[26]

He further states that common sense alone is sufficient to explode this myth. The revolutionary changes which have occurred in our society within the last fifty years have necessitated continual change and readjustment to the demands of daily living. If older persons were severely handicapped in their ability to learn they would never have survived. The fact that a higher percentage of our population is composed of older Americans and that the average life span is increasing, demonstrated conclusively that older Americans have consistently remained involved in the learning process.[27]

The consensus of leading learning theorists is that the decline in learning ability with age is slight and does not have much, if any, practical significance to learning in real life situations. A tremendous volume of scientific research (most of which has been done since 1955) strongly supports this conclusion. Almost without exception, these studies show that, for all practical purposes the older learner is just as capable and efficient as his younger counterpart.[28] Reliable evidence exists which demonstrates that senior adults can continue to be efficient learners well into the eighth decade of life.[29]

## Physical factors in senior adult learning

Most of the physiological studies related to aging have been conducted in the areas of recall of information, primary memory, response rate, forced organization, secondary memory, and interference. These areas test the ability of the learner to absorb, process, organize and recall data on both a short-term and long-term basis. They also test the ability of the learner to perform these operations under varying conditions of rapidity, complexity, and distraction. Thus, they test the physiological processes of the brain involved in the learning activity. It should be noted that these tests deal almost exclusively in the cognitive areas as opposed to the affective, psychomotor, and experimental areas.

In *Learning for Aging,* Dr. David L. Arenberg and Dr. Elizabeth A. Robertson abstract most of the research in learning dynamics as it affects older adults. They conclude that under some conditions (notably information overload, fast presentation, insufficient time to respond, and interference) older individuals do not perform as well as young adults. They point out, however, that: (1) self-pacing by the individuals minimizes or eliminates most of these differences, (2) a greater variability within older individuals exists, with some performing at levels equal to young individuals, and (3) at their worst, these effects can be easily overcome by the instructor in the educational situation.[30] In summarizing his findings from a nationwide survey of current research and educational programming for older Americans, Dr. DeCrow concludes the following:

This [learning ability] is the only area related to the education of older adults with a well-developed body of technical research. Slight declines in various mental abilities, especially, those related to speed, are persistently detected, but they are not of the type or magnitude to have much practical significance in learning in real life situations. Even these deficits cannot be confirmed in experiments with the same persons over a period of time.[31]

He goes on to state that any severe drop in learning ability is almost certain to be a symptom of emerging health problems rather than an explicit result of aging itself.[32]

All research data in either the United States or Europe indicates that there is as yet no known physiological effect on the learning abilities of human beings due solely to the processes of aging. Other factors, such as overall health, disease, nutrition, inadequate early education preparation, cultural bias, and so forth, can have a profound affect on learning abilities in older individuals.[33] It must be noted, however, that these factors also have much the same effect on individuals in all age groupings. They may be more evident in older individuals, but this is probably due to increased exposure time coupled with a decreased ability to regain full health after illness.

Given normal health and adequate educational preparation, the older American is physiologically capable of learning anything within the range of his individual talents and desires.

## Psychological factors in senior adult learning

Adult educator Malcolm Knowles presents four main assumptions which are necessary to understanding the adult learner. They are:

1. Changes in self-concept. As a person matures, he moves from total dependency to total self-directedness.

2. The role of experience. As a person matures he accumulates a deep body of personal experience which he uses as a core for relating new experience.

3. Readiness to learn. As a person matures his readiness to learn increasingly is dependent on his personal tastes and goals.

4. Orientation to learning. As a person matures, his concern and interest shift from subject-centered learning to problem-centered learning.[34]

Analysis reveals that these assumptions are especially true of the senior adult learner. Contrary to popular belief, the older person seldom reverts to total dependency and in general has a deep desire for independence.[35] The older learner has a vast pool of experience from which to draw and therefore is highly selective in relating new experience to it. What has often been called rigidity is more likely to be high selectivity in learning. The older learner better knows what he needs to know, and what he does not need. The older learner is also less amenable to learning subject matter just for its own sake. He must first feel an unmet need or desire within himself in order to be motivated to learn.

Thus, if the older learner is involved in a learning activity which allows self-directedness, utilizes his personal experience as a resource, is oriented toward his inner goals, and is basically problem-centered, he will experience few psychological limitations on his ability to learn. However, as Dr. Knowles points out, when any one or all of these are not utilized in the learning activity, he will experience a psychological tension between his self-concept and the role which is being forced on him. "His reaction is bound to be tainted with resentment and resistance."[36] This negativeness becomes a very real psychological limitation on the older individual's ability to learn. If the older learner perceives the situation as nonproductive or threatening to his self-concept, he is likely to withdraw from the learning altogether. If the act of withdrawal itself is too threatening, or if other (nonlearning) needs are being met, he may remain in the learning activity but appear rigid, negative, opinionated, disinterested, withdrawn, and so forth.

Another major factor particularly related to the older learner is the physical learning environment. The older individual is particularly susceptable to temperature, lighting, sound intensity, seating, and so on. If physically uncomfortable, he will very quickly become psychologically uncomfortable. Usually the environment places a more severe limitation on the learning ability of the older learner than it does on any other age group. The older learner thus should be allowed to self-regulate the total physical environment in which the learning activity takes place.

By far the most important factors with which the older learner must deal are the limitations he places upon himself. In *How Adults Learn,*

Dr. J. R. Kidd states that this is one of the main limits to human growth and development. He further states:

There is the real, practical limit of one's maximum ability or potential capacity. And there is the no less real psychological limit which each man places upon himself. Unfortunately, it would seem that the barriers that most restrict and hobble us, the chains that bind most severely are those which we fashion for ourselves.[37]

If the older learner believes that "you can't change human nature," or "you can't teach an old dog new tricks," or "old people always become senile," he is virtually assured of failure if and when he ever starts a learning endeavor. He begins a self-fulfilling prophecy, for if he believes he is severely handicapped due to his age, then he will, in all probability, be severely handicapped. The older learner must overcome both his own fears and hesitancy and the inherent prejudices of his culture if he is to realize his full learning potential.

Other psychological factors have been categorized by Dr. Howard McClusky as functional needs.[38] He isolates five basic needs which are particularly strong in older individuals. These needs are briefly abstracted below and will not be repeated in chapter 4 (psychological needs).

1. Coping needs. These bottomline needs must be satisfactorily met in order to function in daily living. In a hierarchy of needs they tend to be dominant.

2. Expressive needs. These intrinsic interest needs are met when the older person can creatively express himself, and often for no other reason than this.

3. Contributive needs. These are the giving needs. These are met in the blending of usefulness, acceptability, and service to others.

4. Influence needs. These are the power-over-circumstances needs. Often such factors as retirement, less income, declining health, lessening flexibility, and so on, lead to a loss of personal power on the part of the older person; however, his need for personal power increases during this period.[39]

5. Transcendence needs. This is probably a category of needs almost unique to older individuals. These needs are involved in the realization

of approaching death and the deep desire for ultimate fulfillment—the desire to go beyond the limits of self.[40]

The interplay of these needs will profoundly affect the older learner's desire, readiness, and ability to learn. Almost without exception, his involvement in the learning process will come from the tension of one of these unmet needs.

One of the lesser known and often overlooked psychological aspects of older persons as learners is differentiation. Dr. John W. Powell states that there are three principle differences between children and adults. He says the adult, "has had *experience* of living as a responsible member of the adult world; he has fashioned a *situation* in which his responsibilities are well-defined; and he has solidified some phases of the *self-knowledge*, or at least the *self-picture*, which will govern his actions from now on."[41]

These three aspects increasingly become more evident as the person grows older. Thus, a youth shares more in common with other youths than a thirty-five-year-old with other thirty-five-year-olds; the fifty-five year-old person shares much less in common with other fifty-five-year-olds, and so on. McClusky reinforces this view by stating that the conclusions of his research show that as persons' ages increase so do the differences between them. Thus, in looking at the older adult learner, categorizing and grouping are extremely dangerous. The older learner must, almost of necessity, be studied on an individual basis.

Briefly stated, differentiation is that individuality and uniqueness tend to be more pronounced, both within and between persons, as chronological age increases.

## Pedagogy, andragogy, and geriogogy

The consensus of most contemporary adult educators is that the adult mind is radically different from the child's mind. Thus, his learning goals and behavior are different, necessitating different teaching methodologies. One of the recognized problems of both adult and senior adult education is the frequent use of pedagogic methodology. Teacher-oriented, authority-oriented, content-oriented, formally structured, competitive methodologies are contrary to the basic psychology of the adult, and especially the older adult. As previously discussed, when involved in this environment the adult learner often withdraws from the learning situation or stays as a passive negativist.

Central to this discussion then is the question, "Is there also a qualitative difference in the psychology of the senior adult mind?" If the answer is yes, then a geriogogy (that is to say, a special methodology for older learners) is necessary. This concept is common in Europe and at least implicitly operating in a great many senior adult programs in the United States.[42] After an extensive survey of the research, Dr. DeCrow states:

> The learning psychologists assure us that the physiological or neurological processes of learning do not differ significantly once they are fully established in childhood . . . . Most older adults can learn what they need and desire to learn, subject to the normal dispersion of aptitudes and disabilities in any age group.[43]

Thus, older learners require nothing more than a basic application of andragogical principles coupled with a working knowledge of the principles of differentiation.

*Senior adults and Christian education*

The research data on learning and aging provide basic support for the thesis that God has designed human beings to be continuously growing, developing, and reaching for higher levels of Christian maturity. The later years of life are designed to be, not a time of decline and despair, but rather a time of integrating a lifetime's experience into a deeper spiritual reality. Dr. Harry C. Munro, professor emeritus of religious education at Texas Christian University, states that as the Christian matures the self increasingly takes control, and character develops out of a constant ethical appraisal of personality. He states:"The object of Protestant nurture is not merely to propagate a faith; its object is also to enable persons to develop into reality their highest potential character and worth through embracing that faith."[44] He goes on to say that the goal of the Christian learner is embodied in a person—Jesus Christ. Christlikeness is the goal.[45]

Consequently, it is easily seen that God has designed the later years to be those in which the Christian can be closest to this goal; to be most like his Lord. Thus, the older adult learner is to be treated with the highest reverence, love, and respect.

## Memory

Although memory and learning rely on the same mechanism which is underlying, they are different. *Learning* may be described as "the acquiring of general rules and knowledge about the world." *Memory* has reference to "the retention of specific events pinpointed by a given time and place."[46]

Experimental studies have not demonstrated any clear-cut evidence of memory loss in healthy senior adults. When losses are found, they usually can be explained by the presence of mental and physical disorders. The same has been shown to be true in regard to intelligence decline.[47] Obviously, some senior adults do experience short-term memory loss, but this should not be construed as synonomous with aging.

"Doctor, I seem to be getting more and more forgetful lately."

"How long have you had this problem?"

"What problem?"

Through the years many senior adults have expected to become forgetful as they get older. Then, expectations may gain the authority and strength of moral standards. To not meet expectations may be an indication that their judgment about the future is inaccurate and thus they are poor prognosticators. Better to have judgment affirmed than to have a good memory. Forgetfulness is a stereotype that is commonly accepted as a sign of advancing age. The psychology of this stereotype has been employed by many senior adults who need an excuse to not participate in a particular activity. They can conveniently "forget" to attend. Old people remember what interests them. I never heard of a man forgetting where he buried his money (Cicero).

There is much truth in Cicero's statement, but some older people do forget where they have hidden their treasures. So do youths. Many senior adults who do not have a good memory for recent events may never have had a particularly sharp short-term memory. They may suddenly start thinking that they are losing their memory because they cannot remember things that have just happened whereas this condition has persisted through the years.

As Cicero implied, a selective memory loss exists in senior adults. Experiential studies are not needed to prove that persons remember best what they value and have interest in. If the present is filled with unimportant and unchallenging events then they are not remembered. A nonstimulating environment may drive one to revel in the past. Because of a past that has been expanding with important relationships and events, it may become more important than today. Often, for many senior adults, the future may hold no particular promise.

Some have thought that the tendency for older persons to reminisce indicates trouble with recent memory. Sister Michael Sibille, a practical specialist in gerontology, scoffs at these negative reactions about reminiscing. She reminds her listeners that all of us repeat those life experiences that have been of great joy and interest to us. She compares the brief and often unexciting history of a child to that of a senior adult. The child has much to look forward to and the senior adult has much in the rearview mirror.

Robert N. Butler, head of the National Institute on Aging, in concert with Myrna I. Lewis, provided a new perspective on reminiscence.

The tendency of the elderly toward self-reflection used to be thought of as indicating a loss of recent memory and therefore a sign of aging. However, in 1963 one of us (R.N.B.) postulated that reminiscence in the aged was part of a normal *life review process* brought about by realization of approaching dissolution and death. It is characterized by the progressive return to consciousness of past experiences and particularly the resurgence of unresolved conflicts which can be looked at again and reintegrated. If the reintegration is successful, it can give new significance and meaning to one's life and prepare for death, by mitigating fear and anxiety. This is a process that is believed to occur universally in all persons in the final years of their lives although they may not be totally aware of it and may in part defend themselves from realizing its presence. It is spontaneous, unselective, and seen in other age groups as well (adolescence, middle age); but the intensity and emphasis on putting one's life in order are most striking in old age. In late life people have a particularly vivid imagination and memory for the past and can recall with sudden and remarkable clarity early life events. There is renewed ability to free-associate and bring up material from the unconscious. Individuals realize that their own personal myth of invulnerability and immortality can no longer be maintained. All of this results in reassessment of life, which brings depression, acceptance, or satisfaction.

The life review can occur in a mild form through mild nostalgia, mild regret, or tendency to reminisce, story-telling, and the like. Often the person will give his life story to anyone who will listen. At other times it is conducted in monologue without another person hearing it. It is in many ways similar to the psychotherapeutic situation in which a person is reviewing his life in order to understand his present circumstances. As part of the life review one may experience a sense of regret that is increasingly painful. In severe forms it can yield anxiety, guilt, despair, and depression. And in extreme cases if a person is unable to resolve problems or accept them, terror, panic, and suicide can result. The most tragic life review is that in which a person decides life was a total waste.

Some of the positive results of reviewing one's life can be a righting of old wrongs, making up with enemies, coming to acceptance of mortal life, a sense of serenity, pride in accomplishment, and a feeling of having done one's best. It gives people an opportunity to decide what to do with the time left to them and work out emotional and material legacies. People become ready but in no hurry to die. Possibly the qualities of serenity, philosophical development, and wisdom observable in some older people reflect a state of resolution of their life conflicts. A lively capacity to live in the present is usually associated, including the direct enjoyment of elemental pleasures such as nature, children, forms, colors, warmth, love, and humor. One may become more capable of mutuality with a comfortable acceptance of the life cycle, the universe, and the generations. Creative works may result, such as memoirs, art, and music. People may put together family albums and scrapbooks and study their genealogies.

One of the greatest difficulties for younger persons (including mental health personnel) is to listen thoughtfully to the reminiscence of older people. We have been taught that this nostalgia represents living in the past and a preoccupation with self and that it is generally boring, meaningless and time-consuming. Yet as a natural healing process it represents one of the underlying human capacities on which all psychotherapy depends. The life review as a necessary and healthy process should be recognized in daily life as well as used in the mental health care of older people.[48]

It is highly possible that the created lethargy of a supposedly unexciting environment and a dubious future do not have to be common afflictions for those in Christ. A Christian view of life does away with the tyranny of psychological time. The myth of time can best be understood when a day is seen as a thousand years and eternity is seen as existence rather than the passing of time.

A loss of recent memory cannot be documented in a majority of healthy senior adults for another very practical reason. Death is more of a reality for this age group than any other. Each thought and sensory experience, however limited, because of this may be enjoyed to the fullest. Veterans returning from the front lines have reported a similar experience as they faced the possibility of death. Each conversation, each relationship, and each morsel was enjoyed to the fullest when memory separation from these earthly pleasures became a strong possibility.

In summary, investigations of senior adults as to losses in short and long-term memory have not been negatively conclusive. The research has included an assessment of the possibility of different storage capacities for the young and the old; differences as to information, organization, and depth processing. Depth processing is a concept used to describe the depth at which information becomes increasingly meaningful. Findings in this area seem to indicate that senior adults do not process information to deeper levels as do young people. Thus, durable memory traces are not laid down for easy retrieval.[49] However, one would certainly have to question the meaningfulness of much of the material presented in tests. Two researchers, F. I. M. Craik and S. White, have postulated that older persons may have a problem with the retrieval of information rather than the depth of processing information. They had subjects, old and young, perform four different tasks on sixty-four words with sixteen words used for each task. The tasks were to determine whether the word was capitalized, whether it rhymed, what semantic category (animal, vegetable, mineral) the word belonged in, or they tried to remember it for recall. On free recall, older subjects did poorer but on recognition they outperformed younger subjects in two tasks. Thus, these researchers claim that the results indicate a retrieval problem rather than depth processing. The results are presented in Figure 1.

The reader will need to remember that the information shown in this figure is cross-sectional test results. Although positive in several areas, they do not prove that the older subjects declined or improved in memory because of age.

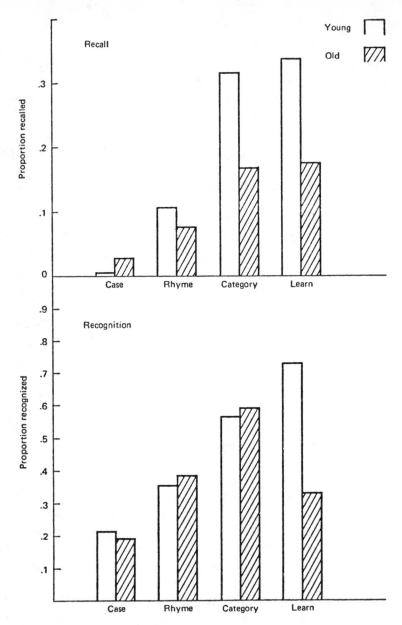

Fig. 1. Proportion of words recalled and recognized following four different orienting task conditions.[50]

Experimental studies of aging, brain function, and memory are limited with human beings because of obvious ethical issues. Animal research has been substituted, but such efforts, even with positive findings may not be reliable when they are related to human beings. Studies of this type have shown only slight losses in memory function. In some tasks, especially less complex tasks, oldsters excel. In more complex tasks of memory they may lose ground. However, even when losses were indicated, intense retraining overcame deficits in the most complex tasks. Several researchers have not considered these deficits the result of memory loss, but performance loss.[51]

In studies of the above type, researchers found such slight losses that might be attributed to aging until other possibilities were explored. For instance, oldsters placed in an enriched environment for one year did much better on their tests. Again, suspicions have been raised as to the physical condition of older subjects. Seldom were the experimental studies bolstered by extensive physical evaluations.

The entire field of psycho-gerontology has evidently made a value judgment in regard to memory. Almost universally we agree. A good memory is a valuable asset. Yet, there are times when memory loss may be invaluable. From a Christian perspective forgetting has been heralded as essential for forgiveness and a bulwark against a grandiosity over past achievements. Memory loss may avoid the destruction of a fragile psyche. (Memory loss is discussed further in chapter 6.)

## Attitudes

Attitudes have been assigned by many psychologists as the principal determinate of behavior. As a result, a variety of personality tests employ attitudinal statements to determine attitudes about a host of subjects. The prediction of behavior in relation to these subjects can be made from the results.

Beliefs, mainly intellectual (cognitive), have not been given the weight of attitudes in determining behavior. *Believe* as found in John 3:16 of the King James Version of the Bible is usually changed to *trust* through Greek studies. *Attitude* is a construct that refers to a mental state of readiness that has been derived and organized from experi-

ence.[52] Certain qualifications must be added to clarify this limited definition. A durability is experienced in attitudes. No, they are not un-
changeable but according to their intensity are resistant to change. This
fact may account for what has been termed the "rigidity" of senior
adults, whether true or not. Attitudes are related to issues upon which
people disagree. They should be distinguished from habits, and so forth.
The most important distinguishing feature of attitudes is that they are
evaluative or affective (feeling). Beliefs are almost always included in
attitudes ("Pollution is dangerous."), or they may be largely unrelated
to attitudes ("Many factories require fuel-burning systems for
energy.").[53] The reason is that a belief usually must have an emotional
element that makes it either negative or positive for it to be a part of an
attitude.

*Attitudes about death*

Within recent years literature about death and dying has become
mountainous. Studies of attitudes of people of different ages and different life circumstances about death have been collected. This has been
true in regard to attitudes of senior adults toward death. Because of the
fact of limited life expectancy one would think that fear of death would
predominate in this age group. A reasonable hypothesis would be that
those who have a limited life expectancy will in the majority fear death.
The studies of fears of death tend to focus on attitudes toward death as
the state which "follows" cessation of life, or as the cessation of life.[54]

Studies of the attitudes of senior adults toward death are fairly
specialized. J. M. A. Munnichs, a Dutch psychologist, has made a
substantial review of this literature. In 1966 in *Old Age and Finitude* he
presented seven systematic studies which help us understand the orientation of senior adults to "the end." The author added his own research
to his findings.

Munnich's contribution and review of seven studies were attempts to
answer the question, "Do most elderly people have a strong fear of
death?" One hundred Dutch elders (seventy years of age and beyond),
served as his sample. From his research Munnich derived the following
attitudes toward death:

1. Only seven were in fear of "the end."

2. The most frequently observed orientation was acceptance (forty out of the one hundred).

3. Acquiescience was another common orientation (twenty-one of the one hundred).

Less than one third of the sample failed to come to terms with their death. The most important conclusion was that only seven were in fear of "the end." Also, the most mature elders were most likely to acknowledge death positively.[55]

Weisman and Kastenbaum reported on an experimental study of patients at a geriatric facility. In spite of the relatively poor health of the patients, an orientation of acceptance was more prevalent than apprehension. Even when patients entered the preterminal phase of life, the main orientation was not one of fearfulness.

Studies by Wendell Swensen, Frances C. Jeffers, Samuel D. Shrut, and recent longitudinal studies at the Duke Center for Aging have provided results that suggest that death fears are not pervasive among the elderly. The variety of research methodologies used to demonstrate the lack of death fear could be used as proof that senior adults are very fearful. However, authorities have chosen to take the data at face value recognizing research limitations.[56]

All evidence seems to indicate that senior adults are less afraid of death than those in other age groups. They may have arrived at an understanding of the quotation found in London's Festival Hall: "And the end of our exploring will be to arrive to where we started and to know the place for the first time."

*Attitudes about grandparenthood*

Grandparenthood is a time for change and a second chance. Whereas strictness and rigidity might have been in vogue when their own children came along, leniency has now gained ascendancy. The state of being once removed from responsibility, blame, and moment-by-moment wear and tear works wonders in changing attitudes toward child-rearing. This is not an uncommon change. Also, the change from benign gray-haired angels who can be abused with grandbaby-sitting chores is fast becoming a reality. They can no longer be saddled with unannounced child-keeping chores and the like. Various writers suggest that grandma and grandpa prefer short visits and private time to pursue their own interests.[57]

A tendency appears for grandparents to attempt to buy the affection of children and grandchildren rather than through an intense effort to become actively engaged in their day-to-day upbringing. Since 1900, a longer span of time brought about by longevity, has increased the likelihood of more people becoming grandparents. This fact may account for the lessening of family reunions. There is less need for horizontal relationships made up of cousins of the same age bracket. Now, there are more four-generational families with single family units gathering for reunions. Often, the grandparents may pay most of the expenses of the vacation time get-together.[58]

Bischof reported on a study by Bernice Neugarten of how middle-class grandparents felt about their grandchildren. She found that the most frequent pattern was that of the grandparent-grandchild relationship as fun-seekers. However, the fun-seeker relationship was seen more in those who were under the age of sixty-five than in those who were over the age of sixty-five.[59]

Recently, a friend of mine sent me a paper filled with paragraphs written by elementary-grade children in response to the question, "What do you think about older persons?" Most of the responses were positive and almost all included a statement about having enjoyable walks with older persons, usually their grandparents. The desire for this walk with grandchildren must be in the hearts of most grandparents.

My grandson when you have older grown
I'll take you to a lake I've known
At midnight, noontime, dusk or dawn.
I want to show you where I've gone
To find my freedom . . . And I want to be
In a boat with you and have you see
And learn from me, oh grandson of mine,
How to cast a fishing line.

For I've been young and too well I know

The rocky road your feet must go.
But I know, too, a path that clings
To a wooded hill where the bluebird sings.
Where dogwood grows, and oak and pine,
And all I ask, oh grandson of mine,
Is to row that boat for you some day
Along that shore where the willows sway
To be with you when first you feel
A leaping fish unwind your reel.

I want you to sleep, as I have slept
Beneath the heavens' reach, star swept.
I want the dawn's first gold betide
To waken something deep inside.
I want you, my boy, to learn to take
Your troubles to a shining lake
. . . and lose them there.[60]

It would be unfair not to include a poetic portrait of grandmothers of many years ago. A youngster would scarcely recognize such a grandmother but many of our readers will. Charlie W. Shedd included it in his book, *Then God Created GRANDPARENTS and It Was Very Good.*

Grandmother, on a winter's day,
Milked the cows and fed them hay,
Slopped the hogs, saddled the mule
And got the children off to school;
Did the washing, mopped the floors,
Washed the windows, and did some chores,
Cooked a dish of home-fried fruit,
Pressed her husband's Sunday suit,
Swept the parlor, made the bed,
Baked a dozen loaves of bread,
Split some firewood, and lugged in
Enough to fill the kitchen bin;
Cleaned the lamp and put in oil,
Stewed some apples she thought would spoil;
Cooked a supper that was delicious
And afterwards washed up the clothes,
Mended a basketful of hose;
Then opened the organ and began to play,
"When you come to the end of a perfect day."[61]

*Miscellaneous attitudes and perceptions*

Richard A. Kalish, an outstanding author in the field of aging, has reminded us of a significant monograph titled *The Myth and Reality of Aging in America.* It was published in 1975 by the National Council on Aging and the Harris polling organization, which conducted an extensive study of older Americans. This study is by far the most extensive ever conducted to determine the public's attitude toward aging and their perceptions of what it is like to be old in this country and to document older Americans' views and attitudes about themselves and their personal experiences of old age.[62] The delineation of public attitudes about aging and the attitudes of the aged have been, in large measure, derived from this excellent survey.[63]

The public at large recognizes that senior adults are a much larger segment of our population than they were ten to twenty years ago. The general public perceives them as being better off in health, education, and finances. However, these accurate perceptions are accompanied by a myth that people over sixty-five are mostly isolated, sitting most of the time, and living within themselves. Actually, the older population is much more active than is imagined. Sixty-two percent of the public see senior adults as sitting and thinking. Thirty-one percent report that they do.

Regardless of the slightly positive perceptions of the public, the young and old have negative expectations of senior adulthood. Although senior adults have been sold this bill of goods, they do not believe that this is their personal predicament. Seniors see this predicament in others and not themselves.

The study revealed that 81 percent of the public agreed that the federal government should support senior adults with general tax revenues. As to mandatory retirement 86 percent were in opposition. Of those responsible for hiring and firing, 87 percent perceived that employers discriminate against senior adults and make it difficult for them to find work because of their negative attitudes about aging. However, 76 percent of the public agreed that senior adults should be able to have a comfortable living regardless of their earning capacity in their younger years. In fact, 97 percent of the public believed that social security payments should be increased periodically to match the rising cost of living. However, this attitude may be changing as predicted by Harold L. Sheppard.[64] Again, 62 percent perceived that most senior adults do not have enough money to sustain themselves while only 15 percent of the elderly found this a personal problem. Yet, as in other instances, they agreed that this was a problem for senior adults in general, but those surveyed thought they were exceptions.

Fifty percent of the public surveyed considered senior adults were frightened about crime. Seventy-nine percent of senior adults did not think this was a problem for them personally.

Only 36 percent of senior adults reported that they spend considerable time watching television. Almost twice as large a percentage of the public, 67 percent, believe that senior adults spend a lot of time watching television.

Over half of the public considered "becoming old" as a dated phenomenon, such as reaching sixty or seventy years of age. Other ideas of "becoming old" were identified with retirement, health, and "it depends."

Older adults (40 percent) have a better self-image of usefulness than does the younger public (20 percent). Only 21 percent of the young public views senior adults as having a "very useful" function in life. Thus, senior adults have projected, in the majority of instances, the negative reactions of society on their peers and still consider themselves bright, alert, and useful. Older blacks have a less positive self-image than do older whites.

Young and old agree in their perceptions of the ways in which senior parents and grandparents assist their offspring. However, they disagree as to the matter of advice-giving. The younger public believes that senior adults give far more advice than they will admit.

Young and old agree that senior adults do not receive proper respect from the younger public. Blacks sixty-five and over perceive this more than do older whites (60 percent *versus* 43 percent).

Most senior adults are interested in volunteering their services. Approximately 6.6 million are either involved in volunteer services or want to be. But they are not satisfied with the giving of full-time to uncompensated volunteer services. They feel that valuable work should entitle the worker to compensation.

## Sensorimotor Skills and Aging

Sensorimotor skills have to do with the speed of an individual's response to sensory stimuli. In this instance, we are concerned about how aging affects this skill in senior adults. The process is very complicated and involves not only the external sensory capacities (seeing, hearing, touching, smelling, and tasting) but other internal sensory organs in muscles, tendons, joints, and those which regulate blood chemistry and other conditions of the body. The elaborate process of reacting to stimuli (external and internal) has been judged to trigger three steps of reaction:

1. The perception or sensing of an event or force that has occurred.
2. The decision as how to respond to the stimulus.
3. The actual response to the stimulus.[65]

Countless experimental studies of reaction time in different performances, multiple performances, difficulties of performances, interference, spatial transpositions, continuous performance, performances with physical and mental deficits present, and numerous other variables.[66] These important studies remind me of the brass instrument studies of Wilhelm Vundt in the first psychological laboratory in 1875 in Leipzig, Germany. Many modern psychological studies rebeled against this limited view of man and moved away from attempts to explain man's psychological condition by examining small parts of him isolated from an awareness of the whole person. This tension between highly specialized examination of discrete units of behavior and an understanding of the whole person will ever be with us. Modern experimental psychologists can now demonstrate the slowed reaction time that is seen in the majority of senior adults. However, this must not be construed to be the consequences of physical deterioration. Also, it is not necessarily negative. If so, speed of response would be arbitrarily assigned positive value for human beings. Many animals respond much more rapidly than human beings and sometimes with destructiveness. The enjoyment of a job well done, caution, and muscular loss either by aging or disuse may be several of the countless factors allowed for a slowed response. Regardless of the causes and evaluation of decreases in speed of sensorimotor responses of senior adults, the condition does exist. Obvious implications are seen in relation to need for preparation, ample time to monitor, simplicity, industrial jobs that demand speed, and in driving in hazardous situations.[67]

## Summary and Conclusions

We have looked briefly at various psychological elements as they are related to senior adults. The process of psychological aging is highly individual. What might be considered as deficits may be assets when viewed within the context of a Christian psychology. The way psychological functions are viewed and employed does relate significantly to the next chapter, "Psychological Needs." These needs may be judged to be out of reach by the senior adult if he sees himself as severely limited in psychological functions.

We have also seen that it is a mistake to look at a living soul through the narrow window of one psychological function. To do so would be to lose sight of the compensatory blossoming of other talents that are possible. Also, it would seriously limit the activity of a living God who assists.

Again, we are not fully aware of the physical regenerative powers of the human organism. This phenomena is seen in the possibility of the restoration or regeneration of sensory functions.

NOTES

[1]Genesis 2:7.
[2]Walter F. Daves, *A Textbook of General Psychology* (New York: Thomas Y. Crowell, 1975), pp. 435-36.
[3]Ibid.
[4]Ibid.
[5]Ibid., p. 437.
[6]Ibid., p. 436.
[7]Paul B. Baltes and K. Warner Schaie, "The Myth of the Twilight Years," *Psychology Today,* March 1974, p. 35.
[8]Baltes and Schaie, "The Myth of the Twilight Years," p. 36.
[9]Ibid.
[10]Ibid.
[11]Ibid.

[12]Ibid., p. 36-37.

[13]M. L. Lieberman, "Psychological Correlates of Impending Death: Some Preliminary Observations," *Journal of Gerontology* 20:182-90.

[14]M. L. Lieberman, "Observations on Death and Dying," *Gerontology* 6 (1966 Study):70-73.

[15]D. B. Bromley, *The Psychology of Human Aging* (Baltimore: Penguin Books, 1966), p. 294.

[16]Baltes and Schaie, "The Myth of the Twilight Years," pp. 35-36.

[17]James D. Manney, *Aging in American Society* (Washington, D. C.: U.S. Government Printing Office, 1974), pp. 47-48.

[18]James E. Birren, *The Psychology of Aging* (Englewood Cliffs, N.J.: Prentice-Hall, Inc., 1964), p. 48.

[19]Manney, *Aging in American Society*, p. 48.

[20]*Hattiesburg American*, 13, August 1978, sec. D, p. 12, quoting from an article by Joseph J. Rizzo in *Seventeen* magazine (August 1978).

[21]Trygg Engen, "Taste and Smell," in *Handbook of the Psychology of Aging*, eds. James E. Birren and K. Warner Schaie (New York: Van Nostrand Reinhold Company, 1977), pp. 559-60.

[22]Ibid., p. 560.

[23]Dan R. Kenshalo, "Age Changes in Touch, Vibration, Temperature, Kinesthesis, and Pain Sensitivity," in *Handbook of the Psychology of Aging*, p. 562.

[24]J. F. Corso, "Sensory Processes and Age Effects in Normal Adults," *Journal of Gerontology* 26 (1971):90-105.

[25]Kenshalo, "Age Changes," p. 562.

[26]Roger DeCrow, *New Learning for Older Americans* (Washington: Adult Educators Association Publishers, 1975), p. 12.

[27]Ibid., p. 11.

[28]Ibid., pp. 12-44.

[29]James A. Thorson, *Psychology of Aging.* Unit 2 in the series of monographs: Profiles of Aging—Gerontology Readings for Health Professionals (Omaha, Neb.: University of Nebraska Medical Center, 1978), p. 13.

[30]Stanley Grabowski and W. Dean Mason, eds., *Learning for Aging* (Washington, D.C.: Adult Educators Association Publishers, 1976), pp. 2-31.

[31]DeCrow, *New Learning for Older Americans*, p. 12.

[32]Ibid.

[33]Ibid., pp. 12-14.

[34]Malcolm Knowles, *The Adult Learner: A Neglected Species* (Houston: Gulf Publishers, 1973), pp. 45-49.

[35]Grabowski and Mason, *Learning for Aging*, pp. 244-47.

[36]Knowles, *The Adult Learner*, p. 45.

[37]J. R. Kidd, *How Adults Learn* (New York: Association Press, 1959), p. 19.

[38]Grabowski and Mason, *Learning for Aging*, p. 330.

[39]Erik H. Erikson, *Identity the Life Cycle: Selected Papers* (New York: International Universities Press, 1959).

[40]Grabowski and Mason, *Learning for Aging*, pp. 330-38.

[41]J. W. Powell, *Learning Comes of Age* (New York: Association Press, 1956), p. 17.

[42]DeCrow, *New Learning for Older Americans*, p. 57.

[43]Ibid.

[44]Harry C. Munro, *Protestant Nurture* (Englewood Cliffs, N.J.: Prentice-Hall, 1956), p. 65.

[45]Ibid., pp. 92-93.

[46]Fergus I. M. Craik, "Age Differences in Human Memory," in *Handbook of the Psychology of Aging*, eds. James E. Birren and K. Warner Schaie (New York: Van Nostrand Reinhold Co., 1977), p. 385.

[47]Ibid., pp. 414-15.

[48]Robert N. Butler and Myrna I. Lewis, *Aging and Mental Health: Positive Psychosocial Approaches* (St. Louis: C. V. Mosby Co., 1977), pp. 49-50.

[49]Diana S. Woodruff and James E. Birren, eds., *Aging: Scientific Perspectives and Social Issues* (New York: D. Van Nostrand Company, 1975), pp. 146-48.

[50]Ibid., p. 147.

[51]James Walker and Christopher Hertzog, "Aging, Brain Function, and Behavior," in *Aging: Scientific Perspectives and Social Issues*, eds. Diana S. Woodruff and James E. Birren (New York: D. Van Nostrand Company, 1975), pp. 152-60.

[52]Gordon W. Allport, "Attitudes," in *Handbook of Social Psychology*, ed. Carl Murchison (Worcester, Mass.: Clark University Press, 1935), p. 810.

[53]H. J. Eysenck, ed., *Encyclopedia of Psychology* (New York: Herder and Herder, 1972), 1:95.

[54]Robert Kastenbaum and Ruth Aisenberg, *The Psychology of Death* (New York: Springer Publishing Co., Inc., 1972), p. 81.

[55]Ibid.

[56]Ibid., p. 82.

[57]Ledford J. Bischof, *Adult Psychology* (New York: Harper and Row, Publishers, 1969), p. 128.

[58]Ibid., pp. 128-29.

[59]Ibid.

[60]Anonymous.

[61]Charlie W. Shedd, *Grandparents* (Garden City, N.Y.: Doubleday & Company, Inc., 1978), p. 38.

[62]Richard A. Kalish, ed., *The Late Years: Social Applications of Gerontology* (Monterey, Cal.: Brooks-Cole Publishing Company, 1977), p. 57.

[63]"Developments in Aging: 1974 and January-April 1975," in *Report of the Special Committee on Aging, United States Senate* (Washington, D.C.: U.S. Government Printing Office, 1975), pp. 59-61.

[64]Harold Sheppard, "The Potential Role of Behavioral Science in the Solution of the 'Older Worker Problem,' " *American Behavioral Scientist*, pp. 71-79.

[65]A. T. Welford, "Motor Performance," in *Handbook of the Psychology of Aging*, eds. James E. Birren and K. Warner Schaie (New York: Van Nostrand Reinhold Company, 1977), p. 450.

[66]Ibid., pp. 450-496.

[67]Ibid., p. 490.

# 4

# Psychological Needs

Each reader could prepare a list of needs that would possibly be as acceptable as the ones outlined in this chapter. They would be derived from common experience and observations. With each of us involved in frequent periods of introspection personal needs are revealed that would suggest the same needs for senior adults. These personal needs are, in reality, basic needs of all age groups.

As senior adults arrive at the end of the human life cycle, their needs are the needs of all human beings from the cradle and through that last developmental step—death. Of course, the difference of intensity of the need in a particular situation and at a particular time in life is obvious. Again, the manner in which needs are met is usually different in each age group; for example, meeting love needs for a small child is tailored for one in that age group. Yet, there is more specificity required. Not only do different age groups have the same psychological needs, but they are expressed differently, met differently, and are highly individual. This observation moves us much deeper than an understanding of needs that are common to all age groups but needs which are common to each individual, expressed individually, and met individually.

The theory of universal psychological needs has intrigued me since the beginning of doctoral studies. Of course, there are a multitude of psychological needs that appear to be altogether different from one individual to the next, but underneath these seem to be foundational needs. Often unmet surface needs are so poignant and observable that the simple foundational needs are overlooked. Again, the expression of symptomatic and possibly secondary needs may be an effort to get the basic needs met.

The list of basic needs that each of you would provide would probably be expressed in different words. Some of you might suggest identical words, but even though the words are not the same, the meanings assigned may be very similar. Thus, this chapter is an effort to refresh our memories about essential psychological needs that are seen as commonsense needs. You will see that they are interrelated spiritual, social, and mental needs. However, spiritual needs must be expressed from these vantage points. In reality, an extensive listing of physical needs bears on one's mental functioning. These physical needs when met allow for the enhancement of life that can only be found as the deep fundamental needs of growth and life emerge. They may arrive as obsessive and extreme needs because of poor physical care. Or, they may develop as natural, healthy needs which flow from the safety of good physical care.

You can easily see how interesting the subject of needs must have been to a new doctoral student. If God made man with particular needs then the meeting of these needs is the greatest work on earth. Is it surprising to you that within Christ are found the resources that are essential for the meeting of these needs? Oh, I have some reservation about the easy use of statements such as, "Christ is the answer." Yes, he is the answer, but to what question or need? What does he want *us* to do? Do we know how to implement his teachings—his life in our own lives in such a way as to become as beautiful as we were when he first thought of making us. How beautiful it would be if the activities within our families and churches were geared to meet these needs within Christ. The meeting of these needs must not be seen as a sustenance program but as developmental. One side of the coin is the meeting of legitimate psychological-spiritual needs. The other side is the development of Christian virtues that help man to become Christlike.

Although the needs suggested in the following pages are common to all men they may be most intense for many senior adults. Because of the lack of life-support assistance such as proper nourishment, health care, and so forth, the essential psychological needs are often unmet.

A nursing home administrator from Virginia shared an extremely interesting life story which bears on the meeting of basic life-support needs. He told of a man who had entered their residential facility for senior adults. His wife had died and he was out there, alone, and largely unable to fend for himself. He was frightened, sick, and undernourished. During the initial days of his new citizenship in the residential facility, he was withdrawn, selfish, grasping, and filled with the same fears and uncertainty as before his entry. As his basic life-support needs were met and he was assured of caring advocates, health care, and proper food he became more secure. Slowly he began to move forward as the fundamental growth needs began to emerge and be met. Eventually he became the president of the council of that facility! Outstanding leadership qualities emerged along with growth in other areas. When one is preoccupied with finding safety there is scarcely time or energy to realize one's potential.

Only as the psychological needs are met can the life-support needs be satisfied. The meeting of physical needs should be the meeting of the need for love. Thus, the three needs suggested in the following pages, if met, should be the doorways through which all the needs of senior adults can be met.

## The Need to Be Socially Involved

To fully comprehend the significance of this need we would need to be alone for long periods of time. I remember the illustration of an innovative young man who was hired to work at an institution for the blind. In preparation, he wore a blindfold for days in order that he might be able to experience the world of the blind person. Of course, there are some advantages in being alone, even being blind. But we need to grasp the meaning of being separated from our fellowmen for extended periods.

### The need and theology

The emphasis on relational theology helps us in our understanding of this fundamental need. Through this emphasis we become aware of the need of God and ourselves for relationship. Theology has been defined as "a study of God and his relations to the Universe."[1] This definition by A. H. Strong at the turn of the century has found new expressions today with relationships of God with man, man with man, and self with self being the subject matter. Theology is a study of these relationships in reference to a living God.

I am impatient with the view that sees the Creator making man in order for him to be lost, so that he can be saved. All Scriptures are relational oriented because God made man for relationship— relationships that can be fulfilled in relationship to him. From cover to cover the Bible is an account of these relationships. The Ten Commandments are explicitly relational bound. Although the need to be socially involved has untold implications for human relationships, the cornerstone is a relationship with God. The first commandments concern a proper relationship to God, and the others have to do with man's relationship to man. The sabbath Commandment, as well as the others, all imply a proper respect for oneself and care for oneself.

The need to be socially involved had its beginning in the heart of God, and then was perpetuated in his creation. "It is not good that the man should be alone."[2] How appropriate that this fundamental need should be a powerful potentiality in *all* men. If not so, the relationship needs of God would be unrequited. Many would dwell alone because the need would not exist in the lives of others.

The need for social involvement must not be seen as a flaw—a deficit in the makeup of God and mankind. We can only grow in this type of relationship. The creation of man allowed for the expression of the beautiful attributes of God. A parallel opportunity is seen in our relationship with our children and in all social involvements.

The most poignant expression of the need for social involvement may be seen in the coming of Christ. If written words would have sufficed, then he would not have come. But "the Word was made flesh, and dwelt among us."[3] God came to us and has offered a supreme sacrifice in order for us to be related to him, our fellowman, and ourselves in mutually rewarding ways. This seems to be the meaning of our Christian faith.

Senior adults need this relationship with God. Even when others are not near, he is near. However, this Presence should be fleshed out as he was in Christ. For that reason, helpmates, families, churches, lodges, clubs, and every conceivable grouping of persons have come into existence. One of the groups, the church *(koinonia)*, should epitomize this Presence. In fact, all relationships should be characterized by this Presence, but all do not.

*Continued number and variety of relationships needed*

If the fundamental need to be socially involved is fully met, senior adults will require all types of relationships. If you are young, middle-aged, or older and active, then in all probability you have babies, children, youths, older persons, and the others of the opposite sex around you from time to time. Many senior adults do not have this wide variety of relationships which are so essential to an enriched environment. Imagine, you are alone most of the time. Maybe your entire life is being spent with a small circle of older people and they are of the same sex as you are. Can you think of seldom seeing a baby or someone of the opposite sex? To fully meet the need for social involvement, then a variety of relationships should be possible. Quite a number of years ago, I heard an address by the famous death-educator, Elizabeth Kubler-Ross. She suggested that one of the best possible arrangements for a nursing home or retirement facility was to have a nursery school or kindergarten adjacent to it. The sharing and caring through planned exchange should prove to be extremely helpful for both groups.

To be socially involved implies a need for multi-generational relationships and this becomes crucial if senior adults are incapacitated and isolated. Sister Michael Sibille, an outstanding practical gerontologist, related an interesting story about multi-generational contacts in a nursing home where she served as director. A heavily bearded young man had requested an interview with her. When he appeared, she could barely see his mouth and eyes, although his nose did protrude slightly. He began by introducing himself as a college student and as a representative for a rock band that wanted to give a concert for the nursing home residents. Sister Sibille began to wonder about the cost and questioned him concerning this. He responded that the concert was free. An agreement was reached as to the time and date for the concert. Of the 190 residents, approximately 100 attended. Sibille reported she carefully watched the reactions of the residents. For various unknown reasons five people walked out during the concert. The remaining 95 responded in a variety of ways. Some rhythmically tapped their hands on their wheel chairs. Others with arthritic legs and feet moved them to the beat of the music. One nurse commented, "Well, this is one thing I'm sure they heard!" In the days that followed nothing was said about different music, the hair, or the beards. Most of the comments were, "Weren't they wonderful?"[4] Multiplied observations of others and those from personal experience indicate that senior adults are tolerant of inter-generational differences and are more so than their middle-aged children.

The importance of a variety of social involvements to senior adults should not be underestimated. It is easy to do this because of the wide circle of friends, acquaintances, and business relations that we enjoy. Mrs. Ann Carlino, a colleague who teaches social work at the seminary, and I were discussing the plight of many senior adults who have limited involvements. She compared the involvements of most age groups to constantly expanding concentric circles as illustrated in Figure 2.

The limited involvements of senior adults as diagrammed does correspond to a popular theory of aging termed "social disengagement." This decline in social relations has been heightened through the years by mandatory retirement, transportation difficulties, chronic illnesses, declining income, and a host of other interrelated factors. An understanding of this interrelatedness of numerous factors should serve us well as we see how a wide range of social problems usually reinforce each other. This is often true in the gradual isolation and negative disengagement of so many older persons. Some senior adults, the five percent institutionalized, may be much more limited in their relation-ships than is necessary. Diligent planning that is informed by an aware-ness of this desperate need for involvement can certainly lead to much improvement in this area. Many senior adults are now reversing the pattern seen in Figure 2. Second and third careers, transportation support services, foster grandparent and adopt-a-grandparent programs, tours, ministry to the homebound, and countless other happenings are allowing for senior adults to experience ever enlarging circles of relationships.

## The quality of social involvements

A crucial factor comes to the fore at this point and it was the central issue in the discussion that Mrs. Carlino and I had. That factor has to do

# Other Age Groups

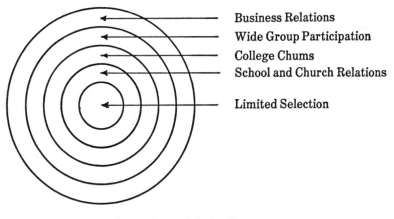

Business Relations
Wide Group Participation
College Chums
School and Church Relations

Limited Selection

# Senior Adults

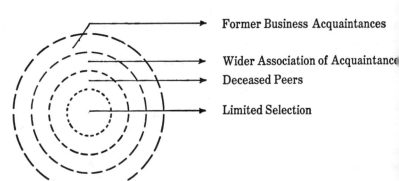

Former Business Acquaintances

Wider Association of Acquaintance
Deceased Peers

Limited Selection

Fig. 2. Involvement of other age groups shown in expanding concentric circles, involvement of senior adults as diminishing concentric circles.

with the quality of social involvements. Senior adults—and for that matter, all of us—do not have the energy to run to all the possible involvements in our social milieu and especially not to the "four corners of the earth." In all probability, largely because of strength and finances, the outreach of many senior adults will be more selective. Why can they not be of such quality as to meet the deepest need for social involvement? They can! However, most of the difficulty may lie with those who are a part of that select group who relate to senior adults. They may not realize the significance and importance that each older person has assigned to them. A patronizing visit that is seen as a duty may be the most glorious opportunity that the senior adult has had in a week, maybe a month, and if you are special-special, maybe a year!

Although we struggle with the idea of determinism (the idea that we are determined by our environment) some truth is found there. Bearing the consequences of our behavior and seeing the results of bad relationships convince us that associations can influence us greatly. Harry Stack Sullivan, an eminent psychiatrist now deceased, said that persons become persons in relationships.[5]

Authorities in numerous disciplines have stressed the importance of relationship in the development of personality. They have either stated or implied that hurt and healing flow out of human social involvements. Almost universal agreement exists as to the importance of the family as the system which provides the most influential relationships, an influence which pervades our thinking and all other relationships—even our relationships with God. No, I am not saying that we are completely bound and determined by them, but we are affected tremendously.

Contrary to popular belief, three generations, in general, have not lived together in one home. Social science research has found that although children, parents, and grandparents usually do not live together, however, a fairly close proximity has been maintained. Also, the idea that children do not visit their aging parents is a myth, but the quality of these relations may be the crucial issue. And when three generational families do reside together certain psychological dynamics are often present.

Henri J. M. Nouwen and Walter J. Gaffney in *Aging: The Fulfillment of Life* have graphically depicted an element of the motivation of much of our socialization with senior adults. They contended that because of a magnification of the plight of many senior adults we might start associating being old with problems. Aging is a fate worse than death and should be avoided at all costs. "Then all our concerns for the elderly become like almsgiving. With a guilty conscience, like friendly gestures to the prisoners of our war against aging."[6] Thus, with our mouths we speak patronizingly with warm tones and great smiles. Pushed aside for the moment are a host of thoughts about the pity and the blight of age. No wonder that the limited select relationships are so unfulfilling for senior adults. Even a child, unable to describe it in words, would sense this double-mindedness. This is the cause of much loneliness, sickness, and fears along the life cycle. They act like they care but something is wrong. They say they love me but something within the eyes, or voice, or gestures seems to indicate reservations. Deep within those eyes beyond the smiling mask is a flashing dart of fear, pity, or something that betrays the countenance.

The fact that senior adults look more seriously at their limited relationships can be documented with hundreds of illustrations out of your life and mine. The lengthy telephone conversations, the willingness to kiss, hug, touch, and countless other signals should remind us of the seriousness of our encounters. Recently, my mother excitedly told me about a friend who was helping her get transportation. She said, "Pearl said that the government was sponsoring a transportation program for older people. Carroll, you know what I'm talking about. It's like that work you did with the Mississippi Council on Aging. Well, I told Pearl that the man who came to pick me up would have to like music!"

Family relationships are often not what they ought to be. Many senior adults are placed under a strain in our society. Living with their children is unacceptable and they are cut off from meaningful relations through retirement and sickness. Thus, they become increasingly isolated from business associates as well as family members. The financial dependency gap that necessitated a sharing of children with their parents has been eliminated through social security, insurance, and welfare. But the severing of dependent relations, a process heralded in American life, also often shatters the emotional dependence of senior adults. They cannot rely on their children emotionally.[7]

Whereas the Mexican-American or Chinese parent would expect not only to live with his children but to receive their continued respect and devotion, older people in our society can expect to be told that they are old-fashioned, that their opinions are out of date, and that their capacity to give helpful advice based on long experience is strictly limited. With our impatience for the future and our restless pursuit of change, the wisdom of an older generation is not likely to count for much. Thus, the rewards of intense planning for the future—if a person lives long enough—follow the law of diminishing returns.[8]

## Dimensions of social involvements

The social involvement need has been examined from several perspectives. This limited presentation of these areas fall within the scope of dimensions of social involvement (relationship). The multi-generational contacts are only one part of the need. The wide range of involvements is another element with the depth of these encounters providing yet another dimension of greatest importance.

These elements of the kinds of social involvements comprise only a narrow selection of those possible. Methods of communication, liking, disliking, confrontation, domination, submission, affection, love, timing, frequency, respect, disrespect, and a host of other elements are important to an examination of all that could occur in the involvements of senior adults. A researcher, Joseph McGrath, has included all these possibilities under three dimensions of interpersonal relationships. These dimensions or parameters are similar to the ones used in our everyday language to describe space. Height, width, depth, and motion (time) are used to understand how far it is to New Orleans and what speed is required to get there by a certain time. Millions of objects with different heights, widths, and depths are in existence. The movements of these objects or persons may travel at a multitude of different speeds which is translated into time. Social involvements, because of their importance, have also been so described in order to understand them better. Of course, the dimensions of space as described above may only be illusions or most assuredly tentative. Some unusually brilliant person may appear on the scene and change our whole language of describing space. It is difficult to even think of such a happening. The same is true for relationships.

McGrath described three dimensions of human relationship: interaction, attraction, and influence.[9] Consider for a moment the innumerable ways of interacting, attracting (either positively or negatively), and influencing each other. Each time that we meet someone we are functioning in these dimensions. In fact, we do not have to meet another person; we function in these dimensions with ourselves. Involvement can be with ourselves. Thus, a more appropriate title for the need discussed in this section could be *extrapersonal involvements.* However, the need to be alone with ourselves at times is an important option in social involvements and would be overlooked if the subject were concerned only with extrapersonal encounters.

It is interesting to broaden our minds to the almost limitless ways of being related to ourselves, others, and God. Yet, this is not enough. The quantity of contacts may be largely superficial or even destructive. At least one outstanding social scientist, Eric Berne, founder of transactional analysis, has theorized that negative strokes from others are better than no strokes. Possibly the value of even negative strokes provides proof of existence, that one has been noted, and gives a person the opportunity to exercise positive responses. At least, one is forced into a response that requires decision. This response may be an opportunity to do unto others as should be done unto us.

*Five Christian principles for social involvements*

If relationships provide a context in which possibilities of growth and deterioration occur then we need to understand how we can improve their quality. Admittedly, even negative strokes may bring out the best in us, but such negative stroking is far from ideal.

The following pages are devoted to a study of five Christian principles which are applicable for all alliances of people, especially senior adults. They were demonstrated by God and are the heart of the relational theology discussed earlier. The supreme model is provided by the Son of God. The principles, in particular, are necessary for family relations, business relations, race relations, church relations, and for relationship with Christ. Any failure to fulfill them may be judged as adulterous.

The principles are biblically and psychologically sound. The Bible is a book largely concerned with these five principles which have also been empirically validated in psychological studies.

Also, the principles should not be regarded as methods or absolute laws that are to be practiced mechanically.

Methods are many

Principles are few

Methods often change

But principles never do.

The principles provide Christian guidelines for all relationships. Wayne E. Oates presented these principles as guidelines for a sex ethic. His suggestion that they are fundamental in all relationships has inspired me to use them as a relationship counseling approach and in other relational contexts.[10] If taken as absolute laws to be religiously adhered to in each human encounter, then the Holy Spirit's assistance and guidance would be unnecessary. The principles have more to do with "being" and "attitudes" than with methods. When practiced dogmatically and pharisaically as were the Old Testament guides, they can be extremely dangerous. You will see the need for this word of caution as the first principle is discussed.

## 1. Knownness *Versus* Anonymity

This first principle may be rephrased as "openness versus hiddenness," and "revealing oneself as opposed to concealing oneself." One can readily see the dangers and blessings that are the potential of the exercising of this principle. Nevertheless, the principle still stands as an absolute necessity if we would grow in our relationships with each other. Reuel Howe, popular author, described this principle as "dialogue," an openness to others with a willingness not only to speak but to respond to what is heard. He considered a distinction was essential between principles and methods in regard to knownness.[11] The beauty of knownness far outweighs hiddenness. However, the careless disclosure of some matters may be fatal to some relationships. My wife has remarked, "Wouldn't it be wonderful if we could live in such a way as to be able to know all about each other." Yes, I agree, and the Bible agrees because it says, "Then shall I know even as also I am known."[12]

*The Bible is a book of knownness.* It is a most vital part of the special revelation of God. How can we relate to one who is hidden? How can we love him or grow in our love for him, if we do not know him? Thus, the Bible is essentially revelation or God making himself—his will—known. He has taken the initiative in creation, in special revelation, and in the word that became flesh.

*Our Father has revealed himself indirectly through creation.* "The heavens declare the glory of God; and the firmament showeth his handiwork."[13] Through mankind, his creation in his own image, we can know God. The highest development of man, enabled by his Spirit, does not approach the attributes of God but certainly gives us evidence of his greatness. That is why Jesus said, "As my Father hath sent me, even so send I you."[14]

*The crowning of personal revelation is seen in Christ's coming.* This Word of God (a word is a vehicle of communication) became clothed in flesh and dwelt among us. At one point in Christ's ministry he proclaimed, "He that hath seen me hath seen the Father."[15] "I and my Father are one."[16] Through Christ we know God, his love, and his perfectness in all ways.

*The principle of knownness is often violated in our churches.* We become mutual admiration societies rather than deal deeply with unfathomable sins and longings. Confession has been turned over to other faiths for so-called "doctrinal reasons." Could this projection about confession have arisen from a fear of self-disclosure? Self-disclosure is dangerous and must be monitored with great care. How well I remember a revival in a southern state! A young woman made a decision of rededication at the close of an evening service. Later, she confessed to her husband that she had been unfaithful to him while he was away in military service. He immediately got his pistol, went to his mother's grave, and wept while he decided whether to kill himself or not.

*The practice of knownness is powerful.* The practice of the principle of knownness in our lives brings about certain consequences. For instance, confessing our faults to one another (Jas. 5:16*a*) allows for the possibility of catharsis, an expression of feeling that may lead toward marital, physical, and spiritual health. The word *catharsis* is derived from *cathartic,* a laxative. Such a purging is cleansing and allows for a more objective review of those things confessed. It may be the first step in forming new resolves and being reminded of the consequences of our behavior. The repeating of shortcomings removes something of the sting and hurt engendered by the holding in of the painful reality of our faults. Sharing it may allow for the diminishing of the burden of the fault by permitting others to get under it with us if it is too large. Also, there is a direct effect in that those who hear may help in many positive ways to correct the flaws which often cause unrest. A variety of reasons compel us to rarely think of senior adults as having a guilt problem. Robert M. Gray and David O. Moberg claim that many senior adults are sent to an early grave because of a burden of guilt. A sense of failure and regret over unattained life goals may haunt them. Some have violated the moral standards of self and society, either in public or in private. Some of their activities may be classified as sinful in social and religious circles. These guilt feelings may arise realistically out of despicable behavior or they may be unrealistic. Such guilt, whether real or unrealistic, is the source of intractable tensions and mental problems unless they are resolved.[17] Through experimental studies with senior adults, "believers" have been found to have a better personal adjustment than do "nonbelievers." A nonbeliever may be bothered by feelings of guilt because of being unforgiven. Yet, all the while contend that he or she does not believe in sin.[18] Thus, the sharing of guilt helps to eliminate its irrational aspects and to work out a sense of forgiveness.[19]

*Knownness is related to love.* Other consequences of practicing knownness are the developments of love and positive feeling. How can we love someone unless we know them? Unless God had made himeslf known how could we have loved him? Intense hostilities may be lessened if we come to deeply know the person against whom the hostilities are focused. Henry Wadsworth Longfellow wrote, "If we could read the secret history of our enemies, we should find in each person's life sorrow and suffering enough to disarm all hostility." The development of the ability to be open with one individual may lead to openness and growing relationships with a widening circle of friends. Also, these open persons may form relationships which may, by reason of proximity, be incorporated into those of the senior adult. Because of this growing openness we can know how to help each other as well as what to expect from each other. The strangeness of relationship is done away with and we become no longer strangers. This knownness usually breeds attraction rather than repulsion. Coca Cola has demonstrated the attraction that grows by a familiarity with a product.

In 1952, a research project had a woman to look at her husband in a tilted room. She exclaimed, "Honey, that's a very funny room you are in. It's crooked."[20] Instead of receiving a distorted view of her husband she saw that something was wrong with the room. This experiment was tried on other couples and it was found that they saw distorted rooms rather than distorted mates. The conclusion of this finding is that when we know people and care about them we are less likely to allow for distortion to effect our perceptions of them. Thus, knowing another person breeds perceptual stability rather than contempt.[21] This finding seems to be particularly applicable for the social involvement of senior adults and the importance of knowing their friends well. Visual and other types of distortions are plentiful enough without having further distortions because of a lack of knownness.

The application of the knowing principle is particularly relevant for the family relationship of senior adults. In regard to husband and wife involvements, Paul Tournier, Swiss psychiatrist, has written an excellent book entitled *To Understand Each Other.* One paragraph pertinent to the knowing principle is as follows:

> The most frequent fault seems to me to be the lack of complete frankness. I see many couples. Behind their difficulties I always discover this lack of mutual openness to one another without which there can be no real understanding. A couple who are courageous enough always to say everything will without a doubt go through many upsets, but they will be able to built an ever more successful marriage. On the other hand, all dissimulating becomes only the portent and the way toward failure.[22]

A good exercise in biblical studies would be an investigation of the principle of openness. The concealment and openness of Miriam, Rahab,

David, our Lord, and countless others provide a wide range of life situations that demonstrate how much understanding is needed in being open.

*Knownness has a significant place in philosophy.* Not only is openness essential from a biblical and theological standpoint, but it is fundamental in philosophy. The word *epistemology* means "a study of knowing." How we come to know this world, especially God, others, and ourselves, is contained in much of the subject matter of philosophy. Different ways of knowing have been suggested. One is *empiricism,* or means of knowing by experimental measures. A large portion of this book has been derived from experimental studies with senior adults. A second means of knowing is *revelation.* One can readily see the significance of this concept in our Christian heritage. A third means is *faith!* Yes, one means of knowing senior adults is through trust just exactly like we come to know God. This belief is extremely important in the social involvements of senior adults. An entire book should be written about the development of trust in the social involvements of senior adults. Faith means unity. Faith is thus a way to deeply know as well as to unite people, particularly senior adults. A fourth way of knowing is by *intuition.* It is generally accepted that this is an attribute that is more highly developed or is a more generous gift in females. Intuition is the knowing of something or someone without a prior knowledge. A fifth means is *rational,* a means of knowing by reasoning processes. At one time, the Doctor of Philosophy degree was a theological degree, psychological degree, and so forth. Thus, these are ways of knowing truth—others are expressed in many types of study and are presented in philosophy as one broad area entitled *epistemology.*

*Knownness is validated in psychology.* As already indicated in theology and philosophy, the importance of openness in psychology is paramount. One of the principal goals in life is to understand oneself. Another is to be known by those who are trying to help us. Thus, the goal of counseling and/or therapy is self-disclosure. Many times we are withdrawn from people, aloof from them because we are afraid that they will spot our weakness. Because of this we avoid people, hide, or are extremely threatened and anxious when they are nearby. Blaming others, rationalizing, overwork, false smiles, and other hiding techniques are used to keep people from seeing us as we are, or think we are. So, a primary problem of senior adults is, can I become known and really know others in my relationships? Will they like me?

Hiddenness is extremely destructive psychologically because we may lose track of who we are. Keeping our thoughts, acts, and feelings buried can make us extremely hostile and confused people. By doing this we increasingly get the idea that we are not worth much if we must keep ourselves concealed. It is something like keeping our worn couch covered. We are ashamed of it. Eventually, we may grow to hate something that causes us so much trouble.

*Health is related to openness.* Openness in social involvements is necessary for good physical health. Modern man is filled with holes. So many emotions are kept buried until they make holes in our stomachs. This hiddenness may literally smother and grip our hearts via the cardiovascular system. The tenseness of being on guard, less discovered, may effect almost all of the systems within our bodies. Dr. Sidney Jourard, author of *The Transparent Self,* has stated that a lack of openness is lethal. He claimed that the reason women live longer than men is because they are much more open.[23]

Women are more open than men, especially the cohort born around the turn of the century. This is amazing since the emphasis on the equal rights amendment for women clearly reveals that women have often not been given the rights of men. Yet, we know that they have talked. They have in the past and still are expressing their feelings. However, younger women who are reared in an environment where women desire and require the same place of responsibility as men may find the results fatal. A legitimate response may be, "Well, I had rather not outlive my husband anyway. If the assumption of responsibilities and the resultant stresses are necessary for dignified existence, give them to me, regardless of the length of life. Quality is more important than quantity." The issue is not responsibility and equal rights, but one's ability to be open and straightforward in a society where openness may mean that you lose your job or find general disfavor from your superiors and colleagues. If the future is filled with ample job opportunities and wealth, maybe openness may not prove to be a problem. Hiddenness may never have been necessary for men to survive in a demanding world. It could have been cowardice.

The knownness principle is given a resounding "Amen" in an article written by Brenda Poinsett entitled "Away from Anonymity."

The elderly need someone to help them escape from their anonymity. Someone is needed to bring meaning to their lives. One story that always gripped my heart is the one of a group of Girls in Action and their leader who were handing out tracts in the community. The leader dropped the girls off at the end of one block and waited for their return. Quickly the girls returned—all but one, that is. They waited and waited for her and still she did not return. As the leader was about to call the police the little girl came running holding out a fifty-cent piece to show her leader. "Where have you been?" the leader anxiously asked.

The little girl answered, "When I stepped on the porch of this one house to deliver the tract, someone said, 'Please come in.' It was an old woman calling; she lived in the house alone. She told me that she had not talked to a single person for two weeks. I just couldn't turn around and leave, so I talked with her awhile. When I did leave, she kissed me and gave me fifty cents."

Do you see the desperation in which some of these people live? Do you see why their greatest need is to have a friend—someone to visit them, to listen, to make them feel important and worthwhile? They want to see somebody. They want to know they haven't been forgotten. Over and over, I hear these words: "We're so glad you came. We're so glad you love us." They are grateful that we care and come to them.

Another comment oldsters make is, "Young people don't pay any attention to us," and it means so much when they do. They like the attention of teen-agers and young adults. One of my volunteers is a college freshman who has a lovely singing voice. She has a good way with elderly people and spends many of her visits singing for them and playing their favorite hymns on the piano. They love it and they love her, but any word from a young person will help. One lady whom I called on one day was overjoyed because the paper boy had taken time to talk with her that day when he was collecting for the paper.[24]

*Openness is a two-way street.* A healthy social involvement between senior adults would require that openness be demonstrated by both parties.

With half a laugh of hearty zest
I strip me off my coat and vest.
Then heeding not the frigid air
I fling away my underwear.
So having nothing else to doff,
I rip my epidermis off.
More secrets to acquaint you with
I pare my bones to strips of pith.
And when the expose' is done
I hang, a cobweb skeleton.
While you sit there aloft, remote,
And will not shed your overcoat.[25]

## 2. Integrity *Versus* Deceit and Duplicity

A second interpersonal relationship principle is "integrity *versus* deceit and duplicity." Basically, this principle can be described as being honest with each other rather than dishonest, deceitful, and two-faced.

After Watergate and literally hundreds of court cases and investigations in government, our appreciation of integrity is growing. The need has been recognized by leaders in the Southern Baptist Convention to the extent that conferences on integrity have been held over the denomination. For example, the deceit and duplicity in the marriage relationship is possibly at an all-time high. Many persons find their marriages going sour at half past the hour. Couples who have lived together for thirty years are looking for greener pastures. Another example is the businessman who takes the risk of selling on credit. And consider the trusting senior citizen. How often he or she is the most vulnerable target in the frontline of rip-offs and confidence schemes. In fact, at times it is very risky to pay for anything in advance—you may never receive the article.

Integrity in an individual is a beautiful sight to behold. Fortunately, my father was that kind of man. Without a doubt, a presence within his life brought together the various potentialities so that you knew he was the same type of man almost everywhere. He was the same at work as at church and the same in our home. This type of wholeness is sought for not only in religion but in all of life—psychology, philosophy, and so on. A simple way of stating it is, "Integrity is when your ought, want, am, and able are all in harmony." Yes, if one knows what ought to be in his life and wants the same thing, then half the battle is won. If he really becomes that because he is able to, then the other half is in place. Such integrity may be found in the lives of senior adults more than in any other age group and may explain what might be termed "a lack of ambition." While serving as an interim pastor in a small church in Mississippi, I heard a senior adult say, "You know, I just don't have too many *wants.*" Some may consider this resignation, defeatism, or apathy. However, I picked up from the conversation a note of peace, a note of having been blessed by God until his cup was running over.

A prominent figure in psychology, Carl R. Rogers, has described for us a person who is congruent. Personal change in people is facilitated when the counselor or another helper, for that matter, is what he *is.* He is genuine and without a "front" or "facade," openly becoming the attitudes and feelings which are inside of him. The term *congruence* has been used by Rogers to conceptualize this condition. An elaboration of congruency may help us to see that when this condition exists we are aware of ourselves, able to live these feelings rather than deny them, and thus, able to communicate them when appropiate. Of course, such a condition is never fully realized in any of us but should exist in some degree if our social involvements are to be meaningful. In clarification, Rogers wrote:

> To give a commonplace example, each of us senses this quality in people in a variety of ways. One of the things which offends us about radio and TV commercials is that it is often perfectly evident from the tone of voice that the announcer is "putting on," playing a role, saying something he doesn't feel. This is an example of incongruence. On the other hand, each of us knows individuals whom we somehow trust because we sense that they are being what they are, that we are dealing with the person himself, not with a polite or professional front.[26]

Within our understanding of God is the idea that perfect harmony exists in the Godhead. In him there is no shadow of turning.[27] He is the same yesterday, and to-day, and for ever.[28] His promises are sure.[29] Such integrity is the foundation of our faith. The genuineness, authenticity, and wholeness exemplified by Jesus inspires the greatest possible trust. That is why senior adults are most comfortable in relationships with him and with others who have Christ as the integrating center of their lives.

The theology briefly expressed in the above paragraph can be seen as a psychological counterpart in the Bible for God's children. In Matthew we find, "Blessed are the pure in heart: for they shall see God."[30] Other verses described those who are not double-minded,[31] have singleness of eye,[32] have set their minds on things above,[33] and love God with all their mind, heart, soul, and strength.[34] Such wholeness and togetherness is an essential element in the social involvements of senior adults.

The implications for integrity in relationships of senior adults are myriad. Trust, dependability, security, and confidence flow out of such trustworthy alliances. Now, we not only know each other, we know that we can trust each other because what we say is what we do. Rather than the cultivation of suspiciousness and wariness through social involvements of integrity we are kept at ease.

### 3. Caring *Versus* Using

A third principle of social involvement is caring for persons rather than using them. Milton Mayeroff has said that caring is the opposite of simply using the other person to satisfy one's needs.[35] Others have contended that the antithesis of caring is apathy. Regardless of the debate that might focus at this point, caring is needed in all social involvements. If it is not present then either apathy or destructive exploitation will exist. Caring is a part of love, the second psychological need to be presented in this chapter. Erich Fromm said:

> Beyond the element of giving, the active character of love becomes evident in the fact that it always implies certain basic elements common to all forms of love. These are *care, responsibility, respect,* and *knowledge . . . . Love is the active concern for the life and the growth of that which we love.*[36]

Caring, an element of love, may be described as actively meeting the needs of another or ourselves, rather than manipulating or exploiting. What an important principle in the social involvements of senior adults! To be used by another or to use someone else has been portrayed as a great crime in the literature of man and especially in the Word of God. We use things but not people!

Caring may be expressed in social involvements of senior adults in two ways. First, caring is an attitude and, secondly, caring is doing. Which comes first is highly debatable in psychology. Some believe that attitudes are essential for constructive behavior and others theorize that behavior/actions engender feelings. Both views are correct to the extent that they do not discount all the validity of the opposing view.

This third principle of interpersonal relationship will be given a more in-depth treatment later. Suffice it to say, when caring is seen as a supreme act of God in Christ reconciling the world unto himself, enough has been said. Rather than exploitation, this was the greatest caring act in the history of man. The beauty of this expression of caring provides a brilliant mirror for us to see the evidences of destructive using which occurs within families as husbands and wives use each other and children exploit and are exploited. Senior adults may use each other and be used by others. It is difficult and maybe impossible to maintain a semblance of relationship when we come to the realization that we are being used. When this realization dawns upon us, the involvement ceases. Such practices, if allowed to continue, are detrimental to the perpetrator as well as to the victim.

"Using" as an antithesis to "caring" is not intended as a denial of the value of constructively using or being dependent on each other. Yes, we can meet our needs through each other and God with a mutually rewarding experience being the outcome, but it should not be an exploitive type of using.

Although social involvements are necessary for life, this principle guides us in the qualifying of these involvements.

## 4. Responsibility *Versus* Irresponsibility

Social involvements should have another essential ingredient—responsibility for the partner. This is the fourth Christian principle to help us in establishing and perpetuating quality relationships. It is easy to say, "We should be responsible to each other in our relationships." It is another thing to question, "What is responsibility?" "When should I be responsible?" or, "Am I only responsible for myself?"

First, we need to start with some idea of the importance of this concept. The principle may be stated as "responsibility versus irresponsibility." In suggesting an opposite or antithesis, we can see better the need for relationship where partners are not irresponsible but assume responsibility for each other. Irresponsibilities abound in marriage, family, race, peer, and work relationships. What a load to try to carry when only one person in the involvement is responsible! How difficult to graduate a child from a coerced obedience to a sense of responsibility for life and society! How disquieting to be linked with a mate, nursing home workers, and peers who are irresponsible! Although they may be classed as relationships, often they are very poor ones. Most of the couples, families, or individuals that I counsel are affected by irresponsibilities. However, we must remember that varying degrees of irresponsibility are present. However, some are totally irresponsible! William Glasser, psychiatrist and author, equates mental illness with irresponsibility. He said, "People do not act irresponsibly because they are 'ill'; they are 'ill' because they act irresponsibly."[37] How beautiful it is when we have the privilege of associating with others who have our welfare in mind as well as their own and who know how to relate in a constructive rather than destructive manner.

William Glasser defines responsibility as the ability to fulfill one's needs, and to do so in such a way as to not deprive others of the ability to meet their needs.[38] Although interpersonal responsibility is implied, this definition is not in perfect agreement with a Christian principle of responsibility. Cain's question, "Am I my brother's keeper?"[39] gives us one of the first clues to a Christian interpretation of interpersonal responsibility. In Galatians we read, "Bear ye one another's burdens."[40] A companion verse appears to be in contradiction. "For every man shall bear his own burden."[41] Here we see the need to be personally responsible for oneself and also to help others when their own strength is insufficient. To know when to do this is complex if we depend on the dim candle of our reason rather than on help from God.

As one can readily see, there are endless difficulties in understanding and implementing the concept of responsibility. This fact caused Milton to leave the discussion of this topic to some little imps of Satan for their relaxation and futile pastime.[42] Regardless of the debates about responsibility in the courts, forensic psychiatry, and in discussions of its development and implementation, most agree that it is an interpersonal necessity. One stark exception stands out in the brilliant writings of Ann Rynd. Her philosophy of objectivism emphasizes that responsibility is toward oneself. Erich Fromm stressed the positive side of being responsible for self and others. He said:

> But responsibility in its true sense, is an entirely voluntary act; it is my response to the needs, expressed or unexpressed, of another human being. To be "responsible" means to be able and ready to "respond." Jonah did not feel responsible to the inhabitants of Nineveh. He, like Cain, could ask: "Am I my brother's keeper?" The loving person responds. The life of his brother is not his brother's business alone, but his own. He feels responsible for his fellow men, as he feels responsible for himself.[43]

Fromm has expressed the concept of responsibility as a Christian would hope to express it. Although the concept has been overworked and some might think "trite," our society would be in shambles without it.

When at the University of Michigan in a workshop on gerontology, I became engrossed in a game which was titled, "End of the Line." A number of those present were asked to participate as senior adults who were attempting to meet their essential life needs. Each individual was tethered to a chair and in his hand he held a small board on which were precariously balanced some objects which could be used in the purchase of life-sustaining resources. If each participant clamored to meet his own needs, he endangered others in the group. The tethers would become tangled and the valuable coins of the game would be lost and thus some would die. It was only when cooperation and a sense of responsibility prevailed that each senior adult had the opportunity to survive. I did not want to play the game in the evening when it was scheduled again. It was just a game, but an empathy developed for senior adults as well as a concern for myself in the future. If the present hyperindividualism increases and we are slow in learning the importance of responsibility toward others, so many may be lost.

## 5. Durability *Versus* Separation and Estrangement

The fifth principle for social involvement is "durability *versus* separation and estrangement." It is a time factor principle. Senior adults know the value of long-term, durable relationships. They have also experienced the abandonment that has at times literally torn their hearts out. Reuel Howe has said that when one is abandoned in relationships, something dies within the individual who is abandoned. Erik Erikson goes further: he contends that something dies in each person.

One criterion for determining healthy people is that they usually have the ability to relate to others for long periods of time. You are familiar with the "butterfly style" of so many—sometimes even senior adults. They flit about from one relationship to another like adolescents in the midst of "puppy love." Feelings are hurt or they do not like the way the other person eats, drives, sneezes, dresses, or talks. Often, very insignificant things cause people to give up on each other and relationships are discarded like dresses and pants that are torn or too tight. They may be just tried on like wearing apparel at a clothing store. People would suffer when this occurs because it is not too difficult for most of us to feel "discarded."

Durability is a beautiful principle proclaimed in our Christian faith. The omnipresence of God may be seen as an expression of this principle of durability. It is clearly expressed in the Great Commission when Christ said, "Lo, I am with you alway, even unto the end of the world."[44] Again, he said that nothing "shall be able to separate us from the love of God, which is in Christ Jesus our Lord."[45] The principle is clearly revealed in the doctrine of the resurrection and in John's Gospel:

Let not your heart be troubled: ye believe in God, believe also in me. In my father's house are many mansions: if it were not so, I would have told you. I go to prepare a place for you, I will come again, and receive you unto myself; that where I am, there ye may be also.[46]

If we only could capture this determination to make our relationships durable throughout eternity. In fact, every person with whom we relate could be seen as one to whom we may relate endlessly. What a difference this would make in the way we treat people. Just think! Before me is a living soul who can live forever!

One can readily see that the length of our relationships is vitally related to knownness, caring, and responsibility. It takes time to grow in knowing each other, as well as in loving each other. Leland Foster Wood claimed that "love is partly a gift of nature and partly a development."[47] The time factor is expressed in this statement as a necessity in the growth of love. The development of behavior and attitudes expressing the other principles or, for that matter, the development of any virtue in relationship requires durability. "Relationships that can stand the gaff of everyday life and the searing intensity of human interactions are not built as quickly as youth (and some of the rest of us) would like to think."[48]

Erich Fromm has expressed the destructiveness of broken relationships sociologically, spiritually, and psychologically. He said: "The awareness of human separation, without reunion by love—is the source of shame. It is at the same time the source of guilt and anxiety."[49]

The destructiveness of human separation has been recounted in numerous· volumes and has been verified by common knowledge. Heartache, homeless and hurt children and senior adults, distrust, and economic deprivation have been the result of a lack of durable relationships.

Jules H. Masserman and numerous other authors have written of anxiety that pervades man's thinking because of his preoccupation with death, the ultimate separation. Masserman concluded that all helping professions have arisen as a result of the fear of death, uncertain relationships, and of being a small, trivial person in this great universe.[50] Restated, these three fears of man: death, alienation, and isolation are significantly related to the principle of durability *versus* separation and estrangement.

Paul E. Johnson, author and pastoral psychologist, reminded his readers of the unpredictable nature of even close family ties. One moment there is love and acceptance and in the next moment there is desertion. In the larger community we may sense indifference. Johnson, struggling for a balance of idealism and realism said, "even as we hope for enduring relationships, we know the shadow of death and separation will overtake us at the end."[51] For many persons, the various biblical expressions of durability have served as reminders of the certainty of spiritual reunion.

## The Love Need

Last week I received a call from the director of the New Orleans Council on Aging. He asked me to deliver the closing address for a preretirement conference for employees of the city of New Orleans. This is my fourth year to deliver the address, "Will You Still Love Me When I'm Sixty-Five?" I look forward to speaking on this subject each year—it is such an important question. We have all been asking questions about love in our own unique ways since we were born. Sister Michael Sibille lists love as the first need. She said:

The need to be loved, you know, sometimes we laugh, we think about the romantic songs—a lot of romantic nonsense. They really aren't, you know. Love really does make the world go 'round. We can't exist without love. None of us. Love is important for our very being. We're born with the need for it. The small baby born—coming out of his mother's womb—he doesn't know words, he doesn't know anything, but he feels, through the senses of his own body, a touch. He knows if that touch is gentle and loving, if it's rude and rough, and he responds in his little body by crying, by getting stiff, if it's a cruel touch. If it's warm and a gentle loving touch, he relaxes, he coos, he cuddles up, he feels good. You've heard of the battered child syndrome. The child who is cruelly treated by the parents, beaten? What happens to that child? I'm not talking about mentally. Physically the child does not grow. The growth is stunted, physically, because the child goes unloved and will not grow without a climate of love. Well, we never outgrow this need. All throughout our lives, from the moment we're born to the very end of that growth cycle when we're old, we need to know in ourselves that we are of value, that somebody, somewhere cares about us, that we're important.[52]

Sister Sibille is correct; for some reason, that mysterious quality of life called *love* may fulfill all needs. Yet there is a need to try to understand it better and especially know how to implement it. That is why I enjoy speaking to the employees of the city of New Orleans.

Whether one quotes Fromm or the Bible, the need for loving must be clearly established. Positive attitudes about love as the greatest interpersonal potentiality must be strengthened. This is especially true for senior adults.

The importance of love in life literally is explicit or implicit on most of the pages of God's Word. The great commandment's verb is love.[53] The new commandment's verb is love.[54] God is love![55] It is placed above the great gifts of mankind—above faith and hope! First Corinthians 13 leaves no doubt about this dynamic that never fails. Why is love greater than faith—greater than hope? Henry Drummond wrote *The Greatest Thing in the World*. It is not necessary for you to ask, "What was his subject?" You know!

William Glasser, psychiatrist, has written about love as one of the basic needs of human personality. However, he does not narrow his view of this need to "our need for love." He moves beyond it to "we need to love." Thus, this primary need has two sides—the need to love and the need to be loved.[56] That is why the heading "love needs" was selected for this section.

Howard J. Clinebell, pastoral counselor and author, has brought these needs together in a succinct statement that persons need to experience authentic love in a dependable relationship.[57]

Recently, Dr. Ray Rust, president of Anderson Junior College, Anderson, South Carolina, delivered the Layne Lectures at New Orleans Baptist Theological Seminary. For three days he spoke on "Fundamentals of Ministry." "Integrity" was the first basic ingredient of ministry given attention. Next, "self-discipline" was considered. Then, it was almost as if everyone knew "love" just had to be the last and most essential element in ministry. Parallel to these lectures, my class lectures were focusing on "Personality Needs That Require We Be Therapeutic Persons." Glasser, Clinebell, Rust, and a host of other professionals see love as the most important element in life. It would be difficult to find genuine authorities in any area of religion, psychology, or psychiatry, that do not stress the importance of this meaningful four-letter word.

While teaching about love's being a basic personality need, I am reminded over and over again of the strength that love gives to me. To be loved gives me the confidence to keep trying even if I fail—because the particular brand of love I receive never fails. I tell my students, "I may fall flat on my face in my teaching, but I know there is someone at

4321 Seminary Place who will love me in spite of this." And, at this time, the verse comes to mind that nothing can separate us from the love of God.[58]

What a relief to know we are loved—not only if we succeed—not only when we fail—but always. We can bear up under the most drastic losses, suffer the greatest physical pain and failure, when we are loved. Is there any doubt that love to give and receive represents one of the greatest needs of senior adults or, for that matter, of any age group. But how exquisite it must be to love when our opportunities to do so may be limited. The intensity of such loving has been experienced by all of us when we have been separated from one we love and we are reunited. The ecstasy of being flooded with feelings and acts of love when we have been deprived and then given opportunity ranks as the highest experience of man and God. Not only in expressing love but also in receiving love are we bathed with a sense of well-being and self-esteem. Imagine the unlimited range of growth possible in such a loving relationship. It needs to be reciprocal. Thus, the need to be loved could never be fulfilled unless the need "to love" is recognized.

Several great theologians, psychologically oriented, have proclaimed that the inability to love is equivalent to insanity. A loveless life is in trouble because of this. Fritz Heider expressed a simple but profound truth that undergirds our thinking when he stated that the true value of an individual can only be externalized when he is loved. He added: "Furthermore, the lover himself reaches his highest value in love.[59]

This discussion of this important need of senior adults brings us to the difficult task of defining love. Also, how do we love? In reality, I have never read a satisfactory definition of love nor would I be so presumptuous as to attempt one. However, I can say that "God is love."[60] No description of love can equal that which is seen in Christ Jesus our Lord. Thus, a description of love and its development is seen in its ideal expression only in relation to Christ. He *did* the Word, *spoke* the Word, and *was* the Word. The heart of that Word is love. I am simply saying that the ideal love that can flood and fulfill us is described by his life and actions. The simple verse, "He first loved us,"[61] takes on unusual significance when we ask, "Can a senior adult love others if he has not been loved?" The answer may be found in the fact that we have been loved first. Most of us are familiar with the Greek word *agape*—a selfless expression of love for others—God-love. Any attempt at loving each other falls short of this ideal. There are many who believe that this greatest expression of altruism is a mirage and to pursue it is like "chasing a rainbow." No doubt, our best efforts at loving are contaminated. Again, certainly we are fulfilled in loving, but maturing love does not spring primarily from a desire for self-fulfillment.

It is important at this point to give attention to a counterfeit love that Abraham Maslow describes as D-love (deficiency love). D-love is loving only because people need love. Our very discussion of "love needs" may lead us into the subtle trap of loving senior adults *only* because they need to love and be loved. No, we must see within each other loveliness, not just a need for love. Many children are smothered into oblivion by a symbiotic false love. Often the love comes from hatred or guilt. This same type of love flourishes in our fears of age and guilt about the misfortunes perpetrated on age. If you love me only because I need to be loved, please do not bother. Love me as a being made in the image of God. Love me because I am me. You can understand what I am trying to say. What I feel and desire at this moment is universal. This quality of love which senior adults need is called B-love (being love). In all probability Maslow discovered this *agape*-like love in his study of one hundred great personalities. And, in fact, most of them were men of religion.[62]

Recently, a doctoral student and I were discussing the rewards of relationships where *agape* love, or some semblance of it, occurred. He suggested that this love could only flow from a fulfilled life. In other words, if we are unfulfilled, most of our efforts are concerned with our unmet needs. We may suck people into the vortex of our swirling needs rather than offer a selfless, giving love, when they are drawn close. Since our needs are often unmet, then it is easy to see how seldom we can offer selfless love. However, sometimes our cup runneth over and at that time we may begin to approach the selfless love that is so healing. However, Maslow found exceptions to the idea that the basic needs must be met before a person could realize a great potential in loving—in self-actualization. He claimed only a general accuracy for the position that basic needs *must* be met, regardless of the exceptions which one may find.[63]

The listing of Maslow's hierarchy of needs has a prominent basic place for "Belongingness and Love Needs." Maslow was appalled that psychology has had so little to say on the subject of love. He said:

> One might reasonably expect that the writers of serious treatises on family, on marriage, and on sex should consider the subject of love to be a proper even basic part of their self-imposed task. But I must report thtat no single one of the volumes on these subjects available in the library where I work has any serious mention of the subject. More often, the word love is not even indexed.[64]

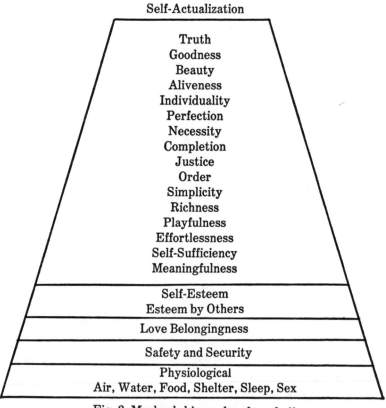

Fig. 3. Maslow's hierarchy of needs.[65]

The hierarchy of needs as described by Maslow has many religious overtones. They are humanistic and focus on self-actualization. His psychology is considered a part of third-force psychology, which views man as a human being as opposed to the view of man as an animal in works of Freud and Watson (Skinner). However, Maslow points to a revisioning of psychology as a fourth force which will be transpersonal, transhuman, centered in the cosmos rather than in human needs.[66]

The importance of love, giving and receiving, must be given the place of highest value if we are to become our best. Yet, there is a greater objective than just becoming our best. At the heart of Christianity is that desire to help others achieve the fullest realization of their potential. Again, the Christian impulse points us to a goal that is even beyond the self and human-other—it is the exaltation of our Creator. As the God-image in ourselves and others is being fleshed out, all eyes must turn to him and our voices proclaim him as Lord of lords. Thus, the balance of self-love and other-love finds a proper perspective under the love for and of God.

Senior adult self-preoccupation is fatal. Love for others and God is the cure. Whether this self-preoccupation is being negative or positive we need to "look away." Look away to hosts of people who run the race of faith before, beside, and after us. We need to look "unto Jesus the author and finisher of our faith."[67] Love helps us to do this. Love is doing this. Directing our attention away from ourselves avoids the hyper-attention that keeps us on center stage. Who can bear the bright hot lights of self-scrutiny all the time? Who can stand before the penetrating glare of others even though we clamor for their attention? Love under-cuts this continued self-analysis and narcissism that fosters fear—fear of inadequacy and rejection. "Perfect love casteth out fear."[68] For the senior adult, true love gives appropriate attention to self but love of others and love of God banishes fears. Who could ask for anything more? Senior adults could face isolation and abuse, but with the power of love, be not afraid. They could walk through the valley and the shadow of death—no fear! Face the inequities of modern life and struggle with the impediments of chronic illness and long months between checks with patience—the patience that love brings! No, I do not understand exactly how love casts out fear in all the situations. The power of this value or God presence or whatever love is, cannot be fully explicated. I could keep elaborating and write beyond the end of this book, but there is more! I want to say simply that senior adults who are facing life's greatest crises need love.

Well, I am not in love with love. It is you, him, myself. The word *love* is not love. People have said it millions of times and love was not present. The word is a symbol and we must get deeper than the symbol if love is to be fully understood. No, I do not mean that the symbol is unimportant but I want the acts of love, the feelings of love, the thoughts of love, and the words of love. That is what senior adults need to receive and give.

Yes, I think we can decide to love but if we have never been loved, it may be impossible. We may not have the beautiful feelings of love, but we can, hopefully, begin to do the acts of love. We can act our way into love better than any other way. I do not believe that love (all the ingredients) comes automatically. Love must be developed. The capacity to love is a gift of God's grace, but the ability to love is developed. Look around you in life and judge for yourselves, "Are not some people seemingly unable to love?" Does not the Bible teach a developmental view of man—that growth in the Christian virtues requires intense efforts? Really, it should be a pleasurable task. And, the ability to love automatically must be counterfeit—anything that does not come from diligent seeking and effort may be worthless. Maybe the time, the struggle, and the vantage point of age allow her the privilege of loving like God has loved us!

## The Need to Be Worthwhile to Self and Others

The need to be worthwhile to self and others is apparently a universal need. It is expressed in the words of William Glasser, psychiatrist and author, as "the need to feel that we are worthwhile to ourselves and to others."[69] Again, it must be stressed that people of all races, creeds, ages, and cultures have the same universal needs. A Chinese infant has the same needs as a king. Although the physiological, psychological, and/or spiritual needs are universal, our Christian ministry has been focused on those needs that are discussed psychologically. The use of "psyche" as "soul" may help us to see the interrelatedness of these needs, although they may be discussed from a psychological orientation.

Being worthwhile to self and to others has particular relevancy for a Christian psychology. The foundational need for socialization must be met before the love needs and needs of worth can be met. However, you may argue that the meeting of love needs is sufficient in and of itself for feelings of worthwhileness. True, love from another accentuates our value and gives us a sense of intrinsic worth, but often very negative feelings flood over us when we are living uselessly and destructively.[70] This need of worthwhileness has been discussed in the films of Sister Michael Sibille as "the need to be useful." Sibille also included a fourth related need of senior adults and entitled it "recognition." These two needs seem to be subsumed under the broader, two-pronged need suggested by Glasser. Also, the need for worthwhileness is vitally related to "purpose" and "meaning." The need for meaning is elaborately spelled out in Viktor Frankl's *Man's Search for Meaning, The Doctor and the Soul, The Will to Meaning,* and *The Unconscious God.* Frankl, a Viennese psychiatrist, through logotherapy (meaning therapy) has provided new horizons for Christian psychology. A brief review of "usefulness" and "meaning" may help us to explicate further the basic need of worthwhileness for senior adults.

## Being useful

Even the most loved among us would begin to doubt our worth unless we have some opportunities to be useful—have something worthwhile to do, something to contribute. Sibille said:

Whatever your job is, you know it's important to you, to society, to the community you're in, to your family. The older people today had a job, maybe the women were just housewives, but somebody had to raise all those kids, wash the clothes, cook the meals, and they didn't have instant food, washers and dryers, and so it was a full day, a hard day's work for them with this family. They were useful. Nobody told them. In fact, if their husband went home and kissed them and said, "Darling, you're useful," she would have slapped him. You know, he could say, "I love you." But not that "You're useful," although she was. Okay, as we get older though, especially this generation, they're not doing things, they're not producing, they're no longer needed by anyone. And all of a sudden you find them getting depressed, feeling very badly, because they don't have anything to do. To me this is the greatest challenge that we face in meeting the needs of older people. It's trying to put back into their life a feeling of usefulness.[71]

Sibille is right, a great challenge exists in helping many senior adults regain a sense of usefulness. Again, the challenge is not totally our challenge, but theirs too. The challenge to recognize the need, clear the way for meeting the need, and sometimes, motivate them may be within our province. Usually, we have so much need to help—we help senior adults into oblivion. Fortunately, many resent this patronizing stance and go about being useful in many ways. A good motto that comes from crisis intervention methods is "Don't do anything for anyone that he can do for himself." Of course, one can get too literal at this point and never express kind acts of assistance. The crucial issue is to not foster dependency or "uselessness."

## The will to meaning

Sigmund Freud started us on a psychological understanding of deep, core tendencies within human nature. He postulated the presence of a "will to pleasure." Adler added what was to him more fundamental, a "will to power." Clinebell emphasized a "will to relationship," with which I have deep agreement, and Viktor Frankl has stressed a "will to meaning." Frankl's theory lends itself to an in-depth analysis of the need to be worthwhile to self and others. In fact, all the above experiences of "will" have relevancy for the achievement of worthwhileness. However, the theoretical psychology that has evolved from them at times is antithetical to Christian psychology. While this is true especially in relation to the ideas of Freud, it is less so as we borrow from the insights of Frankl's logotherapy. Frankl described his therapy as "medical ministry." While so much of psychiatry has been concerned with finding out what is wrong with man, he was interested in helping man discover his meaning in life. When asked about the difference betwen logotherapy (meaning therapy) and the psychoanalysis of Sigmund Freud, he said:

". . . in the first place, can you tell me in one sentence what you think the essence of psychoanalysis is?" This was his answer: "During psychoanalysis the patient must lie down on a couch and tell you things that sometimes are very disagreeable to tell." Whereupon I immediately retorted with the following improvisation: "Now, in logotherapy the patient may remain sitting erect, but he must hear things that sometimes are very disagreeable to hear."[72]

One can readily see the implications for senior adults as they are confronted by life as to their meaning. Frankl, like Glasser, and others within our Christian tradition see responsibility as basic to self-esteem and esteem by others. He saw this search for meaning as a primary force in the lives of all men and age groups and not a cover-up or replacement for inadequacies and sexual needs. He disagreed with authors who hold that this striving to fulfill a unique, personal meaning is equivalent to defensive maneuvers. He said, "But as for myself, I would not be willing to live merely for the sake of my 'defense mechanisms,' . . . man, however, is able to live and die for the sake of his ideals and values."[73] The belief that worthwhileness can only be realized in responsibleness is clearly revealed in his statement:

As each situation in life represents a challenge to man and presents a problem for him to solve, the question of the meaning of life may actually be reversed. Ultimately, a man should not ask what the meaning of his life is, but rather must recognize that it is he who is asked. In a word, each man is questioned by life; and he can only answer to life by answering for his own life; to life he can only respond by being responsible. Thus, logotherapy sees in responsibleness the very essence of human existence.[74]

## A Christian interpretation

The meaning of being called; the idea of talents; the Great Commission; the concept of being a member of the body of Christ with particular functions; letting our light shine; running with patience the race that is set before us; and a multitude of other spiritual truths speak volumes about usefulness, purpose, and meaning. Also, the encouragements of those who applaud; those who rise up and call us blessed; and, the ultimate recognition, "well done thy good and faithful servant" meet this deepest need through our Christian faith. Self-actualization, meaning, usefulness, purpose, and the crowning fulfillment of life can only be realized through Christ. Wayne E. Oates makes no apology for the fact that true selfhood can only be fully realized through Christ.

Even though a radical humanism approximates a massive denial of a sovereign God, we are all vulnerable to elements of this senseless position. At times, similarly to the first of God's creaturely creations, we become expansive in our personalities. The depth psychology of this tendency is enough to keep us busy in our Christian psychology throughout a lifetime. Somehow (much of theology is devoted to these "somehows"), we lose sight of our obvious ignorance and finiteness in the midst of the overwhelming mystery and reality of God's world. We think we can "know all," "do all" and "become all." How fatal! Our very struggle to prove this becomes our undoing because we only accentuate our incompleteness. It resembles the lostness of a small child left alone and the adolescent rebellion of one who is convinced about his premature adulthood. No, we cannot realize our worth, move toward worthiness and value, until we are properly related to "the way, the truth, and the life."[75] He is Christ! One's cosmic insignificance, only one of billions of human beings, is heightened apart from him.

I am a great believer in humanism, Christian humanism! Christ died for human beings with unheard of potentialities residing within them because of the gifts of God's grace. Many people surround us who are noteworthy and are not Christians. Their strength to achieve and reach certain levels of expertise and maturity are the result of the gifts of God's grace. They are not aware of the source of these blessings that fall on the "just and on the unjust."[76] But they cannot find fulfillment, worthwhileness, and meaning apart from Christ.

A beautiful but treacherous turn has been made in the field of psychology. A great, current danger (but old as Adam) must be averted through a Christian psychology. A third-force psychology harkens back to the turn of the century when God was totally imminent and *all* the powers of God were inherent in human protoplasm. I love human protoplasm! Christ was human and my wife is human. But my wife is not God! God is eminent and transcendent. He has created man with marvelous capacities that resemble the Creator, but we cannot "become" without him. This "becoming" cannot be approximated without his gifts and presence. In fact, the preoccupation with "becoming," the fad of modern psychology, is nauseating and anti-Christian when individual development is attempted at the sacrifice of others—and God. It is impossible to "become" outside of community and equivalent to pride outside of a relationship with God. Pride that is an expansiveness of personality is one of our greatest sins. It is on the opposite end of a continuum from sexual preoccupations that constrict human personality and limit intellectual, social, and spiritual development.

I consider the most deceptive expression of "becoming" as that which is seen in some of our "spiritual growth" movements in evangelical Christianity. It appears that the entire goal may often be the achievement of "individual sainthood." The imperative to lose ourselves in acts of love and spiritual concerns is lost under the goal of becoming a spiritual giant.

Great dangers are inherent in a psychiatry, psychology, or religion without a living God. This "God" is not the "individual!" If the individual is "god," then idolatry prevails. L. D. Johnson, professor of religion and chaplain of Furman University, said in a conference on "Psychology and Psychiatry as Religion,"

When psychiatry becomes a religion it becomes an idolatrous system from the biblical viewpoint. Idolatry is whatever replaces the Lord God in one's thought and life. If one's ultimate concern is not concern for the Ultimate, you have idolatry.[77]

Karl Menninger, cofounder of the Menniger Clinic in Kansas City, psychiatrist and author, who is still active and alert at age eighty-five, spoke at the same conference. He decried the perversions and abuses of psychology which have exploited so many for so much money. He said that those psychological teachings that assist a person in elevating his own self-esteem or self-regard at the expense of being a neighbor, visiting people in prison, and considering the poor and children are opposed to Christianity. He added, "The theory of self-ism is to quit thinking about all these things and pay attention to number one. Think how important you are, or how important you could be if you had a little more self-respect."[78]

In summary, the meeting of the three significant needs of senior adults (socialization, love needs, and the need to be worthwhile to self and others) must be met in a relationship with Christ. They must be met from the perspective of the individual's needs but ultimately from the perspective of blessing the lives of others and the glorification of our God.

## Other Lists of Needs

An understanding of the needs of senior adults may help us change our attitudes and behavior toward them. Only three great needs that have a particular relevancy for a Christian psychology of aging have been presented. It would not be fair to the reader or other writers not to, at least, list the needs of senior adults that they consider to be most important.

In a pamphlet entitled "The Christian Family and Its Aged Members," the Christian Life Commission of the General Convention of Texas published an excellent listing of needs that encompass the psychological, physiological, and spiritual.

1. They need to love and be loved. They need friends and companionship.
2. They need to be useful. They need activities in keeping with their ability.
3. They need adequate income for food, clothing, lodging, health, and some miscellaneous purposes.
4. They need recreation along with an opportunity to entertain as well as be entertained.
5. Older persons need to continue to grow through mental stimulation, keeping up with the times and learning new facts.
6. They need physical care. When they are well and active, care means regular examinations to discover problems which may be treated. When they are handicapped, care means rehabilitation and special provisions for them in the home. When they have serious chronic illness or are physically or mentally incapacitated, care may mean institutional service, though such institutional service ought to be the last resort for a Christian family.
7. They need to be an integral part of the normal life of the family, the church, and the community.
8. Most older people do not want to be around their children or grandchildren all the time. They value their privacy very highly and generally prefer to maintain their own homes. The best living arrangements for older people may be with their relatives, but this is often not the case. If it is necessary for an older person to live with relatives there should be mutual agreement that he or she

will not interfere with the parents in their disciplining of their children.

9. Christian families should be aware of the deep spiritual needs of their aging members. The aging especially need the assurance of God's continuing love and protection, release from anxiety about illness and fear of death, a continuing spiritual growth through new experiences with the Lord, and a continuing feeling of usefulness in the work of the Lord. Certainly the greatest need for those who have come to old age without Christ, is to come to a personal acceptance of Jesus Christ as Saviour and Lord. It is never too late to make this decision.[79]

Clark Tibbitts has suggested five needs which should be satisfied if senior adults are to grow:

1. The need for relatedness, or association with others;
2. The need for creativity;
3. The need for security;
4. The need for individuality, or recognition; and
5. The need for orientation or an intellectual frame of reference.[80]

In the *Unadjusted Girl*, W. I. Thomas elaborated on his theory of four wishes. These wishes are suggested as being a comprehensive formulation that would allow for the satisfaction of life if these wishes were achieved. They are:

1. The wish for security
2. The wish for response
3. The wish for recognition
4. The wish for adventure.[81]

An early, widely acclaimed book, *Mental Hygiene,* written by Herbert A. Carroll, of the University of New Hampshire, includes four human needs that have been related to senior adults. They are:

1. The need for physical security
2. The need for emotional security
3. The need for mastery
4. The need for action.[82]

The needs of senior adults are the needs of all age groups. Specific psychological and spiritual needs that have been suggested, if met, seem to indicate the prospects of life that is fulfilled. The greatest resource for meeting these needs is Christ. He has chosen, in the main, to express himself through our interpersonal relationships.

As the needs are reviewed, the various emphases and theories in the field of aging make sense. A study of the needs of senior adults cannot be separated from remembrances of those we know and love. I see my mother and a host of senior adults whose needs are intense and often unmet!

## NOTES

[1]August H. Strong, *Systematic Theology* (Philadelphia: The Judson Press, 1907), p. 1.
[2]Genesis 2:18.
[3]John 1:14.
[4]Sister Michael Sibille, *Psychosocial Aspects of Aging,* Part I (film).
[5]Lawrence C. Little, *Foundations for a Philosophy of Christian Education* (New York: Abingdon Press, 1962), pp. 80-81.
[6]Henri J. M. Nouwen and Walter J. Gaffney, *Aging: The Fulfillment of Life* (Garden City, N.Y.: Image Books, A Division of Doubleday & Company, Inc., 1976), p. 17.
[7]John Papajohn and John Spiegel, *Transactions in Families* (San Francisco: Jossey-Bass Publishers, 1975), pp. 38-39.
[8]Ibid., p. 39.
[9]Perry J. Rushlau and Gary Q. Jorgensen, eds., *Interpersonal Relationships: A Review* (Salt Lake City, Utah: Regional Research Institute Bulletin, 1966), p. 5.
[10]Wayne E. Oates, *Pastoral Counseling in Social Problems* (Philadelphia: The Westminster Press, 1966), p. 102.
[11]Reuel Howe, *The Miracle of Dialogue* (Greenwich, Conn.: The Seabury Press, 1963), p. 40.
[12]1 Corinthians 13:12*b*.
[13]Psalm 19:1.
[14]John 20:21*b*.
[15]John 14:9*b*.
[16]John 10:30.
[17]Robert M. Gray and David O. Moberg, *The Church and the Older Person* (Grand Rapids: Wm. B. Eerdmans Publishing Co., 1977), p. 49.
[18]Ibid., p. 85.
[19]Ibid., p. 195.
[20]Robert E. Silverman, *Psychology,* 2d ed. (Englewood Cliffs, N.J.: Prentice-Hall, Inc., 1974), p. 161.
[21]Ibid.
[22]From *To Understand Each Other* by Paul Tournier. ©M. E. Bratcher, 1967. Used by permission of John Knox Press.
[23]Sidney Jourard, *The Transparent Self* (Princeton: D. Van Nostrand Company, Inc., 1964), p. 15.
[24]Brenda Poinsett, "Away from Anonymity," *Contempo,* June 1974.
[25]Tom Prideaux, unpublished poem.
[26]Carl R. Rogers, *On Becoming a Person* (Boston: Houghton Mifflin Company, 1961), p. 61.
[27]James 1:17*b*.
[28]Hebrews 13:8.
[29]Romans 4:16*b*.

[30]Matthew 5:8.
[31]James 4:8.
[32]Luke 11:34.
[33]Colossians 3:2.
[34]Matthew 22:37.
[35]Milton Mayeroff, "On Caring," in *World Perspectives,* vol. 43, ed. Ruth Nanda Anshen (New York: Harper & Row, 1971), p. 1.
[36]Erich Fromm, *The Art of Loving* (New York: Harper & Row, 1956), p. 26.
[37]William Glasser, *Reality Therapy* (New York: Harper & Row Publishers, 1965), p. xv.
[38]Ibid.
[39]Genesis 4:9*b.*
[40]Galatians 6:2*a.*
[41]Galatians 6:5.
[42]David E. Roberts, *Psychotherapy and the Christian View of Man* (New York: Scribner and Sons, 1950), p. 94.
[43]Fromm, *The Art of Loving,* pp. 27-28.
[44]Matthew 28:20.
[45]Romans 8:39*b.*
[46]John 14:1-3.
[47]Leland Foster Wood, *How Love Grows in Marriage* (Great Neck, N.Y.: Channel Press, Inc., 1961), p. 13.
[48]Lester A. Kirkendall, *Premarital Intercourse and Interpersonal Relationships* (New York: The Julian Press, Inc., 1961), p. 159.
[49]Fromm, *The Art of Loving,* p. 9.
[50]Jules H. Masserman, ed. *Current Psychiatric Therapies, I* (New York: Grune and Stratton, 1961), p. 217.
[51]Paul E. Johnson, *Person and Counselor* (New York: Abingdon Press, 1967), p. 57.
[52]Sister Michael Sibille, *Psychosocial Aspects of Aging,* Part I (film), 1974.
[53]Matthew 22:37.
[54]John 13:34.
[55]John 4:8*b.*
[56]Glasser, *Reality Therapy,* p. 5.
[57]Howard J. Clinebell, *Basic Types of Pastoral Counseling,* p. 18.
[58]Romans 8:39*b.*
[59]Fritz Heider, *The Psychology of Interpersonal Relations* (New York: John Wiley & Sons, Inc., 1958), p. 237.
[60]1 John 4:8.
[61]1 John 4:19.
[62]Abraham H. Maslow, *Toward a Psychology of Being* (Princeton, N.J.: Van Nostrand Company, Inc., 1968), p. 41.
[63]Salvatore R. Maddi, *Personality Theories: A Comparative Analysis* (Homewood, Ill.: The Dorsey Press, 1976), p. 93.
[64]Frank G. Goebel, *The Third Force* (New York: Simon and Schuster, Inc., 1971), p. 41.
[65]Ibid., p. 52.
[66]Maslow, *Toward a Psychology of Being,* p. 30.
[67]Hebrews 12:2.
[68]1 John 4:18.
[69]Glasser, *Reality Therapy,* p. 9.
[70]Ibid., p. 10.

[71]Sibille, *Psychosocial Aspects of Aging.*

[72]Viktor Frankl, *The Will to Meaning: Foundations and Applications of Logotherapy* (New York: New American Library, 1969), p. 152.

[73]Ibid., pp. 154-55.

[74]Ibid., pp. 172-73.

[75]John 14:6*b.*

[76]Matthew 5:45*c.*

[77]*The Baptist Courier,* South Carolina, October 5, 1978, p. 13.

[78]Ibid.

[79]Christian Life Commission of the Baptist General Convention of Texas, *The Christian Family and Its Aged Members.*

[80]Clark Tibbitts, "Creating a Climate for the Middle Years," in *Aging in Today's Society,* eds. Clark Tibbitts and Wilma Donahue (Englewood Cliffs, N.J.: Prentice-Hall, 1960), pp. 318-20.

[81]Ethel Sabin Smith, *The Dynamics of Aging* (New York: W. W. Norton & Company, Inc., 1956), p. 30.     [82]Ibid., p. 32.

# 5

# Psychological Adjustments and Development

## Adjustment

Most psychological textbooks list "adjustment" as a psychological function because it is vitally related to personality development. In my opinion, this is a correct relationship inasmuch as one's adjustment in life has much to do with his personality at the time of the "adjusting process" and with personality changes in and after the "process." However, I have wanted to separate adjustment and personality development for some time. That is why a section in this chapter has to do with the internal developmental aspects of aging rather than a major on external forces. This is to say that we are discussing two sides of the same coin. But the section on development is intended to give emphasis to creative choice.

### Definition of adjustment

Adjustment has been defined as "the efforts of an individual to satisfy his needs as well as to live up to the expectations of others."[1] One can readily see that according to this definition many senior adults may be poorly adjusted because of the inability to meet needs and expectations. Thus, maladjustment, which is really a form of negative adjustment, has been defined as "behavior which does not completely satisfy the individual and social needs of the person, even though it may reduce his drive tensions . . . . Maladjustments, because they represent partial satisfactions of the wishes and needs of the person and because certain of them become ingrained as habitual behavior, impede readjustment.[2] Senior adults may be adjusted in varying degrees from maladjusted to well adjusted.

A simple outlining of the key factors involved in adjustment are:

1. The precipitating event, situation, and so forth, which necessitates some order of adjustment.

Such events or changes which many senior adults experience may include (1) retirement and withdrawal from household management or unemployability, (2) withdrawal from active organizational and community leadership, (3) loss of significant others by death, (4) loss of independence, (5) loss of health, (6) separation from children, (7) loss of sexual prowess, (8) facing agism, (9) loss of income, (10) loss of physical surroundings, (11) loss of roles, (12) loss of multigenerational contacts, (12) closeness of death, and (13) planning in terms of immediate goals. These are only a select number of changes that require adjustments by senior adults. Although they appear to be negative, unwanted changes, this is not the case. Within them the Christian may see the possibilities of challenge and growth.

2. The state of the responding senior adult is a significant factor in adjustment.

The entire history of the individual becomes important as he faces change. Health (physical and psychological), spirituality, intellectual ability, past experiences, and numerous other intrapersonal intangible elements of each unique senior adult affects his ability to adjust.

3. The external resources that are available to senior adults are vital in adjustment.

Finances, significant relationships (church, family, neighbors, and so on), professional resources (physician, minister, lawyers, counselors, social service personnel), transportation, personal advocates, housing, and opportunities to contribute usefully are determinative in adjustment. And, the most important resource is the personal relationship with Christ.

4. A conclusive factor in adjustment is the result.

The shift in the stimulus of change in the senior adult and the change in resources are interrelated in a split-second glimpse of adjustment. The last factor, the results, is to suggest that adjustment is a continual process. However, as each complex situation is presented the senior adult, a measure of stability exists either through maladjustment or a good adjustment.

*Stress and adjustment*

As previously stated, senior adults may make all levels of adjustment between positive and negative adjustment. Part of the adjustment may be helpful while another part is destructive. The goal is to have a majority of positive or constructive adjustment activities. These activities (negative or positive) have been called "habitual patterns of problem-solving," "adaptive maneuvers," "defense mechanisms," "coping mechanisms," "coping skills," and so on. Whatever a senior adult does to meet a life situation is his attempt at adjustment. This is not to say that all life situations are negative. Many are beautiful and positive. Neither is it true that only the stressful or unpleasant life situations have the most dangerous potential. Of course, many stressful situations arise in the life of each senior adult. Often because of decreased physical energy and the possibility of limited resources, they are vulnerable.

Holmes and Rahe have developed a scale demonstrating the impact of various life events. When one views this scale and the assignment of impact power to the various events, the individual must be kept in mind. We must not see each person affected to the same degree by each situation. Yet, we can, on the basis of experimental studies, know that the population in general is affected to this degree on each item. Table 10 will provide a number of clues to the importance of adjusting to change.

Notice those most stressful events that occur in the lives of many senior adults. Holmes and Rahe did not mention that the chart is stacked against them. A number of the most stressful situations seem to cluster in old age. Consider those stressful events that appear in the life of the average senior adult.[3]

1. Death of spouse (100)
2. Death of a close family member (63)
3. A personal injury or illness (53)
4. Retirement (45)
5. Changes in the health of a family member (44)
6. Sex difficulties (39)
7. Gain of a new family member (39)
8. Change in financial state (38)
9. The death of a close friend (37)

## TABLE 10

### The Stress of Adjusting to Change

| Events | Scale of Impact |
| --- | --- |
| Death of spouse | 100 |
| Divorce | 73 |
| Marital separation | 65 |
| Jail term | 63 |
| Death of close family member | 63 |
| Personal injury or illness | 53 |
| Marriage | 50 |
| Fired at work | 47 |
| Marital reconciliation | 45 |
| Retirement | 45 |
| Change in health of family member | 44 |
| Pregnancy | 40 |
| Sex difficulties | 39 |
| Gain of new family member | 39 |
| Business readjustment | 39 |
| Change in financial state | 38 |
| Death of close friend | 37 |
| Change to different line of work | 36 |
| Change in number of arguments with spouse | 35 |
| Mortgage over $10,000 | 31 |
| Foreclosure of mortgage or loan | 30 |
| Change in responsibilities at work | 29 |
| Son or daughter leaving home | 29 |
| Trouble with in-laws | 29 |
| Outstanding personal achievement | 28 |
| Wife begins or stops work | 26 |
| Begin or end school | 26 |
| Change in living conditions | 25 |
| Revision of personal habits | 24 |
| Trouble with boss | 23 |
| Change in work hours or conditions | 20 |
| Change in residence | 20 |
| Change in schools | 20 |
| Change in recreation | 19 |
| Change in church activities | 19 |
| Change in social activities | 18 |
| Mortgage or loan less than $10,000 | 17 |
| Change in sleeping habits | 16 |

| Events | Scale of Impact |
|---|---|
| Change in number of family get-togethers | 15 |
| Change in eating habits | 15 |
| Vacation | 13 |
| Christmas | 12 |
| Minor violations of the law | 11 |

*Note:* Reproduced from an article by Thomas H. Holmes and Richard H. Rahe published in the *Journal of Psychosomatic Research.* Copyrighted by Pargamon Press, 1967.

10. Change in the number of arguments with a spouse (35)
11. Son or daughter leaving home (29)
12. Change in living conditions (25)
13. Revision of personal habits (24)
14. Change in residence (20)
15. Change in recreation (19)
16. Change in social activities (18)
17. Change in sleeping habits (16)

The numbers in parentheses are indicators of the impact of the event (change). The theory behind the scale is that if a person accumulates 200 or more points in one year he will have a resultant physical or mental problem. The cluster of changes listed above could conceivably occur in the life of a senior adult in one year. If this did happen, the impact would be 644! However, the senior adult must not see this impact as inevitable. The theory may be accurate for a large number of our population. An awareness of the stressful potential of change only serves to enhance the value of a Christian psychology. You will note that all the changes listed were not negative changes. The negative impact occurs when the senior adult over-responds in excessive fear, guilt, anxiety, anger, excitement, and so on. The importance of a serenity and balance that comes from a healthy Christian life cannot be underestimated.

Many of the changes listed above as related to senior adults are seen as losses. When confronted by too many changes, most may respond very poorly. Seligman presented evidence from a study of 4,500 widowers that illustrates this point. For a period of six months after the death of their wives, 213 of the men died. This number was 40 percent higher than the anticipated rate for that particular age group. After the first six months, the rate returned to normal.[4]

Most knowledgeable people are aware of the implications of stress for physical problems and even death. Some always want to find a physical cause for physical problems. There may be a physical cause, but often behind it is the psychological stress.

Avery Weisman says:

> The concept of a "psychological death" arouses antipathy among layman and scientist alike. Our cultural bent is to blame death on organic factors, even if a few abnormalities can be found. Nevertheless, it is absurd not to recognize that psychological forces may alter the psychobiological medium. Not only are so-called psychosomatic illnesses very common, but the onset of various unquestionably organic diseases can be traced to such psychosocial events as bereavement, depression, (and) despair.[5]

No doubt, all change (positive or negative) brings a measure of stress. Since life is constantly changing then no escape from stress can be found. It would be difficult to see how that change could be realistically dealt with were it not for an experiencing of its weight. However, the crucial line of demarcation is when the tension is destructively intensified. If handled correctly, the stress should decrease, but if allowed to continue and intensify, major damage may be done to the individuals. Also, others may become affected by the spin-offs that occur in relationships.

Stress usually produces negative connotations. It may be defined as a strain; pressure; force that strains or deforms; tension; strained exertion. Often stress is considered as tension. However, Hans Selye, an author of note on the subject, disagrees with the idea that stress is tension.[6] He, like other psychologists, views stress more in terms of change, whether negative or positive, rather than strain or tension. Dr. Tim LaHaye wrote, "The natural struggle for existence will automatically cause emotional shifting which produces changes in behavior and, in some cases, changes in appearance."[7] Dr. Thomas Holmes, professor of psychiatry at the University of Washington School of Medicine, states that "change, whether good or bad, places stress on human beings."[8]

Since stress is viewed by scientists as perennial then each reaction by the individual must be seen as the stressor. Stress cannot be avoided.

Even while fully relaxed and asleep, you are under some stress. Your heart must continue to pump blood, your intestines to digest last night's dinner, and your muscles to move your chest for respiration. Even your brain is not at rest while you are dreaming. Damaging or unpleasant stress is distress . . . . In common parlance when we say someone is "under stress," we actually mean under excessive stress or distress.[9]

### Crises and adjustment

Stress as a cause of physical and mental illness has been clearly documented. "In the body, as in a chain, the weakest link breaks down under stress although all parts are equally exposed to it."[10] People have been aware of the illness-producing effects of stress for a long time; but research, narrowed to a "stressful illness" focus, is fairly recent.

The role of stressful life events in the etiology of various diseases has been a field of research for the last 25 years. Derived from William B. Cannon's early observations of bodily changes related to emotions and Adolph Meyer's interest in the life chart as a tool in medical diagnosis, the field was first given formal recognition at the 1949 Conference on Life Stress and Bodily Disease sponsored by the Association for Research in Nervous and Mental Diseases. Since then several groups of investigators have adopted this general framework in independent long-term projects.[11]

The relation of attitudes or mental functions to our physical health is seen clearly at this point. Physical and mental stress is difficult to separate because of the unity of the living soul. The permeating effect of stress or change, regardless of the direction from which it comes, affects all persons physically, socially, psychologically, and spiritually. The response of the living soul is largely the key to whether stress becomes debilitating distress.

Gerald Caplan and Eric Lindermann, two psychiatrists, have given us a theoretical understanding of what happens when stress becomes a crisis. A crisis is no small happening to persons, especially senior adults. The Chinese have called it a "dangerous opportunity." The Greek word for crisis is *krisis,* which has been given the meaning "to separate." It has been termed a "turning point" in the medical world. A brief definition of crisis is "an upset in a steady state." Caplan and Lindemann were the first to systematically research this dangerous yet opportune phenomenon. Out of a crisis can come deterioration or growth, and, at the least, a person may return to his former state. However, as has been indicated by the analyses of Holmes' and Rahe's scale of stressful changes, the senior adult has prospects for numerous crises in a brief span of years. How he or she copes with these events determines much of their future.

Fortunately, many senior adults, especially devoted Christians, are professionals at meeting and conquering hazardous situations. They have been there before and almost welcome the opportunity to do battle with the most serious threats that are found on the battlefield of life. Others may not be able to face these crises in a constructive manner and thus enter into a decline.

Recently, I was surprised when a loved one, known for her love of life, a heartiness, slipped over beside me and whispered, "Carroll, I want you to sing "How Great Thou Art" at my funeral. I cried as I put my arms around her and assured her that I would if that was what she wanted. She said, "My darling has gone on to be with God, and I don't want to live any longer." It was not difficult to see her depression and recognize the changes that had occurred in her life since the death of her loving companion. Regardless of the supports and assistances that are placed around an older person who is left alone, such a situation can be extremely difficult and hazardous. What I saw on that Sunday afternoon in the face of this eighty-year-old loved one was the aftermath of a serious crisis.

Changes, stresses, and crises may be seen as psychological shocks. Some changes or stresses may be slight but must not be underestimated in the accumulative power. Those changes and stresses that have the greatest potential in becoming a crisis have been isolated for brief review. To know something of the possibilities of potential crisis events is to undercut some of their power for destructiveness. The shocks or adjustment tasks outlined in the next few pages are generally considered to be universal tasks. However, they are experienced in a highly individual fashion. This is especially true for senior adults because the length of life has much to do with differentiation. The longer a person lives the more of a distinct individual he becomes. Thus, with the shocks of life being the same, the individuals affected are not. Some senior adults may become ill and others will not.

Some people develop chronic diseases and psychiatric disorders after exposure to stressful conditions, and others do not. Exposure to stressful situations alone is almost never a sufficient explanation for the onset of illness in ordinary human experience, and other factors that influence their impact require consideration.[12]

Two important factors that have much to do with determining the consequences of psychological shocks are mental attitudes and physical resistance. "The way you face the crises and trials of life often determine your state of health."[13] Thus, the implications for a Christian psychology of aging are enormous at this point.

## Adjustment Shocks

### Unemployment

Unemployment is a psychological shock. Retirement from one position may not be the same as a loss of employment. Retirement may be shifting from one marketable position to another marketable position rather than retirement from life. E. L. Bartz suggested that "retirement from a skill does not mean retirement from society."[14] Loss of employment usually has negative connotations and may subsume desired retirement, forced retirement, replacement or firing, or loss of job by sickness. Even desired retirement is a psychological shock. Unemployment has numerous negative and positive psychological implications.

### Loss of income and possessions

Approximately 25 percent of senior adults are poor. In fact, senior adults are the only persons, in general, who *get* poor. Others who experience poverty are born into it. Senior adults compose slightly more than 10 percent of our population but make up 20 percent of the poor in America.[15]

There is little doubt of the relationship between extremely limited income and mental disorders. One study found psychiatric problems to be more prevalent among the lowest class as compared to the upper classes. Another study revealed mental disorders were related to lower income and educational levels.[16]

Studies are not needed to pinpoint the reasons for the relationship of psychological problems and loss of income. Anyone who has tried to meet the necessities of life such as housing, adequate diet, medical care, transportation, and so forth, with a limited income has felt the stress, distress, and often crises of this embarrassing situation. Several sociologists declare that most marital problems of young couples stem from inadequate income. Consider the implications for senior adults and the family disorganization that may occur.

A measurable and obvious loss most often seen in unemployment is a loss of income. Income may be seen as vitally related to the maintenance and acquisition of possessions. Money itself is often a prized possession that because of its powerful symbolism is equivalent to possessing reality. A loss of money and its power is similar to a loss of self. Our possessions are extensions of ourselves. Because of this psychological truth it is suggested that senior adults who are moved to nursing homes or other residential facilities should be allowed to take with them certain prized possessions. A lack of financial ability to restore and maintain home, automobile, garage, shrubbery, and lawn may be tantamount to self-deterioration. The loss of possessions would seriously effect one's ability to maintain leadership in the community and the larger family. Dinners for the extended family; gifts for the children, grandchildren, and others; limited nutrition; changes in quality of clothing are all losses of possessions that may allow for the development of an insidious depression or loss of self-esteem. These losses may be anticipated and even turned into positive factors if one feels justified in not being able to meet the preemployment expectations.

## Loss of status

Viktor Frankl has suggested three values in life in hierarchical fashion. At the bottom, but nevertheless a great value, is creative value.

This value, or activity of great worth, is achieved by creating, making, or producing something. The focus of one's entire life may be at a desk in an office, in the farm fields, in a pulpit, or in one of the countless other work situations which come to mind. At these stations of work many senior adults have derived a sense of importance or status. If one views his work as the main reason for status in the eyes of others and his own, he may be right. However, the sense of a loss of status to this type of person will be traumatic. At present, this is particularly true for many senior adult men and a lesser number of women. Women usually have two jobs if they are employed in the labor market and continue in the often rigorous task of housekeeping. Thus, when they are unemployed, they still have the responsibilities of home. Many have only regarded their employment out beyond the home as supplementary. However, these dynamics are rapidly changing and for younger female cohorts the loss of employment may be as serious a change as it has been for males.

The loss of an opportunity to make a significant contribution at work each day may be a severe blow. Many see the dawn of a new day as a chance to begin anew at work. A kind of reparation or restitution may be planned each morning, when one heads out for his daily task. "I'll be able to make up for many of my failures today." "If I do better at work today, I'll feel better about myself." Countless similar statements are made consciously and unconsciously as the work day is faced. When uncertainties and insecurities exist, the opportunity to use one's work in the alleviation of guilt is lost when unemployment comes. Of course, employment may be the source of dissatisfaction or guilt, but the hope that this condition can be rectified may be lost also.

One can readily see how loss of employment is related to self-worth. The present bias about age makes such a loss seem final or permanent for some, especially for those who have constructed their entire lives around a particular vocation. Such a loss may remind most of us of similar losses that we have experienced all along the life cycle. I remember directing the graded youth choirs of a very large church when I was in my early twenties. When the members saw the need for a full-time director of music for the entire church music program, I lost my job! I am not sure about all the reasons and dynamics of the situation, but I do remember that I was hurt! You will not be bored with many more illustrations out of my life, but I am aware that losses similar to the loss of employment can affect one's sense of well-being and esteem. It is difficult to construe mandatory, institutional retirement in any other way than "I'm not capable of doing the job as well as it should be done."

## Loss of selfhood

One's particular vocation has much to do with one's selfhood, especially as a Christian. Wayne E. Oates has differentiated selfhood from identity with the former being a narrowing of focus on the individual.[17] This selfhood can hardly be thought of apart from one's vocation. When an individual is asked, "Who are you?" he may respond, "I am John Doe, a carpenter." The seriousness of vocation is heightened by a sense of calling and, thus, because of a loss of employment one may consider himself to be severely damaged. He may consider himself not to be the same legitimate self without a vocation.

## Trends

Harold L. Sheppard from the Upjohn Institute for Employment Research spoke insightfully to a trend in retirement policies. Statistics used were dated from 1959-1969. His observations and assumptions have proven to be correct and will help us understand senior adults in relation to retirement in the future. Also, we can predict fairly accurately the behavior of those of the working population who are not senior adults. Sheppard demonstrated through statistics that the educational gap between older workers and younger workers is narrowing. This narrowing gap is shown in Table 11.

Sheppard's predictions about the outcome of this trend was based on three predictions:

(a) Work will continue to remain a basic source of identity and self-image.

(b) Education affects self-concept and expectations from others.

(c) There are limits to the extent to which the working-age population will want to pay for decent living standards of a growing retired population.[18]

His prediction was that the narrowing educational gap between younger

**TABLE 11**

**Median Schooling of Older Labor Force Members**
**as Percentage of Median of Younger Members**
**(1959 and 1969)**

| | | Median Schooling | | A as |
| | | 45-54 (A) | 25-34 (B) | Percentage of B |
| --- | --- | --- | --- | --- |
| Males | 1959 | 10.4 | 12.3 | 80.0 |
| | 1969 | 12.2 | 12.6 | 96.8 |
| Females | 1959 | 11.7 | 12.3 | 95.1 |
| | 1969 | 12.3 | 12.5 | 98.4 |

Source: Manpower Report, 1970, Table B-11, p. 256.

and older workers would result in a resistance of retirement by senior adults. This resistance would be reinforced by an unwillingness of the younger working population to support an insurance program needed to support retired senior adults.[19] These dynamics are present now and may be anticipated for the future.

*The gift of retirement*

Liliane Giudice has written a beautiful little book entitled *The Gift of Retirement*. The book is a chronicle of her unspoken conversations on the first day of her husband's retirement. Even though the author was born in Paris and now lives in Baden-Baden, Germany, I was thrilled to see the common experiences which we all share all over the world. It would be too difficult to improve upon her description of "His Calling."

Something I do almost every day: I light the candle in our old, bent pewter candlestick. During the evening it often burns on our table between our books and newspapers. But now it seems to me as though the simple white candle lights us to celebration.

What happened today? Almost nothing: You said hello to a couple of people, helped a blind man, bought a book, played a record. Almost nothing happened, and yet much: silently the two of us have grown richer. We will preserve our good thoughts and our good things, lighten our ballast, make ourselves trim and strong, that we may pass unburdened from this way of life to the next.

For this purpose we were granted something wonderful: today. We no longer say "then," but "now." This moment *now* is our treasure, not the next. With the tiny stirrings of the moment we grow toward maturity, even if the strength of our bodies ebb, for we shall lay aside this body at the final change in our way of life.

The desire that tempts us with illusions—a better job, greater success, more money—desire that is only a scourge and never fulfillment, we shall not regret. A "great day" we are unlikely to experience—it might easily be a lost day—but within us something much more powerful is stirring. We experience in the quiet hour that we are part and parcel of God's creative plan, not "then" but now. At this moment you stand before Him active, even if you have left the world of human labor. What does your work for the company amount to, measured against the tasks that may yet come your way today? You are an integral part of a process from which you can never be cut off. He who created you has need of you for the fulfillment of His work. What matters is not your position, your honors, your money—you yourself are required.

We must not seek contentment in "We have done it," or wallow in self-pity in "We have been written off," or think "We have escaped once more" when we have merely taken the easy way out overlooking the fact that what is demanded is our involvement, not our comfort. No, we must present ourselves to today with the strengths and talents that are given us; then our day will be adapted to the ongoing work of God. No longer hired by men but called by Him—how rich we are! Or is it presumptuous to believe that we are not useless, that we can cooperate in the plan of creation? We always have some strength to offer, strength of body or of spirit, of experience or of kindness, and were we crippled or chained to our beds, we would surely have love to offer, gaiety and intercession. In His eyes we are never poor and never old. A source of annoyance? A burden? Hardly. When you are old and sick and in people's way and they push you aside, He who created you will snatch you up. To retire means to take up God's calling—what joy that we can experience it together, that we can help each other to grope our way to Him!

Our retirement is not a decline, but an ascent to God.[20]

If Liliane Giudice's words mean to you what they mean to me, we will never be the same again. What a beautiful part of a Christian psychology on aging.

Often as a result of retirement and unemployment senior adults see themselves as being in the way of others, just useless junk!

## God Don't Make Junk

God don't like junk but we do . . .
We love junk food
And treasure our trash, piling it up in attics, basements and garages.
We love antiques and pay high prices for
   old pots and furniture that grandma threw
   out years ago.
We love everything old, Lord, except ourselves.
We only like ourselves young.
The only junk there's no market for are people!
   the physically handicapped
   the forcibly retired worker
   the obsolete elderly waiting to die.
How come they're not collectible, God?
Why don't they bring high prices at auctions?
It's pretty clear we don't want them around us.
Is it because they remind us that we have to
   grow old too?
Is it that they remind us of our own handicaps,
   our own imperfections?
The way some of us try to appear perfect, you'd
   think we are trying to play God instead of
   ourselves.
We forget that Helen Keller was blind and mute,
   that Beethoven was deaf,
   that Einstein had trouble with simple math.
Lord, help us to face the blindness in ourselves,
   the thousands of times a day we are deaf to our own
   needs and the needs of others.
Give us the courage to confront our own limitations,
   to accept our imperfections,
   to say again and again that we are human, not divine
   and that being human has got to be good enough—
   has got to make us brothers because we are growing
   old—together.
Help us to love ourselves, Lord, so we don't turn each
   other into trash.
You don't make junk, God—Why should we?[21]

*A time to retire*

Daniel J. Levinson reminds me in his book, *The Seasons of a Man's Life*, that in late adulthood it is time for a man's off-spring to assume the major responsibility and authority in the family. He says, "If he does not give up his authority, he is likely to become a tyrannical ruler—despotic, unwise, unloved, and unloving—and his adult offspring may become puerile adults unable to love him or themselves."[22] He goes on to suggest that a man will experience serious difficulties in his work if he continues beyond age sixty-five or seventy. Levinson believes that to continue in such a fashion is to be "out of phase" with one's own generation and in conflict with the younger generation who should be allowed to assume greater responsibilities. He said:

It sometimes happens that a man in his seventies or older retains a pre-eminent position in government. Names come quickly to mind: Mao Tse-tung, Chou En-lai, Churchhill, Ben Gurion, Gandhi, de Gaulle and John D. Rockefeller. But even when a man has a high level of energy and still, he is ill-advised to retain power well into late adulthood. He tends to be an isolated leader, in poor touch with his followers and overly idealized or hated by them. The continuity of the generations is disrupted. The generation in middle adulthood suffers from powerlessness and conformism, while the generation in early adulthood suffers from the lack of innovation, moral support and tutelage they need from their immediate seniors.[23]

One of the characteristics of aging is the time for the transmission of power, a crucial crisis—like time in the lives of many senior adults especially in the late, late adulthood state (eighty and beyond). Robert N. Butler writes of this transmission of power that is so important.[24] It is possible that this freeing of oneself from exacting responsibilities may be the key to the fullest development of the self—not selfishness.

## Loss of health

Declining health may lead to stress that further complicates health problems. I remember my father's final illness at this point. He was tall, very thin; a man who must have suffered from a heart defect since childhood. He weighed little more than 130 pounds although over six feet tall. At sixty-one years of age, his heart began to fail. I remember carrying him in my arms to the bathroom while the physician tried to provide treatment in our home. Finally, he was taken to the hospital. He had never been hospitalized and although he did not complain, I sensed the great apprehension that must have gripped him. His death followed in a few days.

Dr. T. B. Maston emphasized the importance of proper health care among older people in an article written for *Home Life*. He said:

Someone once half jokingly complained, "The problem with life is that about the time we have learned the rules, we are too old to play the game."

Whether this is true or not, most husbands and wives, as they advance in years, will face the problems that come with declining health. The aging process with ill health inevitably comes. One study revealed that 77 percent of men and women over sixty-five years of age had some chronic illness such as heart disease, cancer, diabetes, or arthritis. It has been estimated that at least half of those who live to be seventy-five or more will be faced with a period of invalidism before death.[25]

A United States Senate subcommittee studying aging found that fear of illness, with the high cost of medical care, was a problem of greatest concern for senior adults. Health statistics reported in chapter 1 demonstrate the incidence possible regarding fears about health problems.

Most authors report that only 4 percent of senior adults reside in extended care facilities. However Robert Kastenbaum and Sandra E. Candy speak of this 4 percent figure as a fallacy:

It seems to us that a very elementary kind of error is being perpetrated here, the sort we teach our students to avoid. Our utilization of these population statistics is often fallacious because we fail to recognize that the *data are cross-sectional.* Knowing how many elders are institutionalized at this moment, no matter how accurate a statement, does not tell us how many people will have resided in extended care facilities at some time in their lives. It does not give us the probabilities for an individual; only a series of longitudinal studies could answer that question satisfactorily.[26]

## Loss of independence

### Too much help?

One of my great concerns about the growing interest in helping senior adults is our overconcern. It has been said that love is so very close to hate—to love fiercely and have that love unrequieted may lead to its opposite. Life is filled with activities that are beautiful and good, but with a slight modification, they could turn into acts of destruction. Thus, eternal vigilance is required unless our best intentions become contaminated with our own needs. Yes, our overconcern in government programs, especially, and the deep need to be needed may mitigate against the senior adult. Mrs. Jones, eighty-five years of age, has been reluctant to be dependent throughout her long and useful life. True, she needed help but not so much that dependency has been fostered. To see hard won independence erode is a sad sight. Slowly she has succumbed to the all-to-willing hands of help and has become helpless.

You may say, "I thought senior adults needed our help." Yes, they do, but it takes skill and understanding even in helping our children who we should know very well. Indiscriminate, scattergun help may be providing exactly what they do not need. The golden rule of crisis intervention methodology must be called to our attention again, "Don't do anything for a senior adult that he can do for himself."

## Cultural or biological?

The complex question, "Is the need for independence in human personality genetic or is it culturally derived?" is difficult to answer. However, independence is generally prized by most people, especially senior adults whose cohorts were born in the early 1900's. Since the need to be worthwhile to self and others is a universal need, then independence is vitally related to this fundamental need. Who feels good about themselves when they are too dependent on others out of choice or forced to be so? I wonder how long peoples of certain political persuasions and nations can remain almost completely dependent on their powerful central governments.

## Independence related to many losses

Most of the adjustment tasks described in this section are related to the struggle to maintain independence. The fears emanating from the loss of income, health, and spouse are particularly related to the fear of being dependent. This fear may be dissected to reveal that the possibility of becoming a little helpless child may become a reality. What we feared most—people will not respect our judgments—will not listen—must speak when only we are spoken to—must beg for what we get—are all within the realm of possibility now. What jeopardy! What a plight! Senior adults remember well those days and present days when children had and have few rights—children are often abused—senior adults are often abused. Within the heart of each of us the desire to return to mother's womb and the desire to reach out for the abundant life exist. side by side. A loss of independence—how fearful—yet, how restful. Restful? Yes, until the forces of nature propel us back into life. How blissful to rest in mother's womb—how intoxicating! But something within me cries out to be a person—to be independent. The balance between infantile dependence and destructive independence is not easy to achieve. Maybe the word that my colleague, Dr. Harold Rutledge, gave me is part of the answer. The word is "interdependence."

## Destructive independence

I have seen an independence in senior adults that is fierce and destructive. Yes, they may have survived out of such fierceness but it is irrational and others have allowed this destrutiveness to continue and may have suffered. Later, you will read about characteristics of senior adults as found in the writings of Robert N. Butler. One of these has to do with the transmission of power. Some senior adults, were they to be standing on the parapet of a burning building, would not let others help them, or would only do so after jeopardizing the lives of others and themselves. This is irrational, destructive independence. It resembles the rebellious adolescent independence that allows a person the grandiose belief that nothing can hurt him—that he is powerful and needs no one to help.

## A portrait of dependency (loss of surroundings)

Imagine a predicament when you are not allowed the choice of what food and when you eat, your roommate, the clothes you wear, the time you get up, and so forth. The furniture in your room is not your own and you are told where to go and when to go. Of course, there may come a time in many of our lives when such dependency becomes a reality but generally it is not a necessity to this degree. Admittedly, some very dependent people have lived or wanted to live in such fashion throughout their lives. For them it is not too difficult, but for others such a condition would be equivalent to death or worse than death. You no longer are allowed to go to the grocery stores and department stores and make choices that are so essential for good mental health. Usually, there are two perpetrators of this crime, the senior adult, and the person who helps him into a state of childlikeness.

## Dependency and anger

Whenever I have seen unhealthy dependency, anger is usually present, conscious or unconscious. The ambivalence that allows a person to get in an unnecessary state of dependency has an element of resentment about human life deteriorating to such a pitiful state. This anger may be directed internally with resultant depression or surface occasionally toward others who have fostered such a deplorable condition. Usually, this anger is short-lived in its outward expression because independence is hard to return to after being dependent. Anyway, people doing things for me may be love! What a rationalization! However, it is not consistent with all the nonverbal communications that accompany the ministrations of those who tend what might be a malingerer day by day.

## Loss of significant others

The senior adult may face life's severest test through the loss of significant others, especially by death. T. B. Maston spoke to the loss of a spouse in the later years. He said:

When death comes to a husband or wife, the one left behind will face one of life's major adjustments. Regardless of how mature they may be in the Christian faith, the days ahead will be lonely. And it seems that the longer a couple has lived together and the more devoted they have been to one another, the greater will be the loneliness.[27]

I know something of this loneliness experienced by the surviving spouse. My mother has lived alone since 1953, twenty-five years of widowhood. During her married life she could not drive because my father did the driving. After his death, her inability to drive added to her isolation. However, soon she set about relearning driving skills and established an extensive route to sell cosmetics. Also, she had to have assistance in the simple act of writing a check. Her ability and determination helped her to learn the skills that should have been learned while my father was still with her. In spite of her ability to learn the necessary survival skills, she has been lonely. Also, other persons have been lost through death or other separating factors. Dear friends have slipped away, sisters and brothers are now gone, Aunt Dottie is now in a nursing home, Mrs. Webb, a precious friend, has moved to California. I hear her speak of these losses with a longing, wistful look. Maybe that is why she suggested that the title of this book be "The Keys to the Kingdom," a hymn that speaks much about the life beyond. "And if Christ be not raised, your faith is vain; ye are yet in your sins."[28] A Christian psychology must make a place for a Christian destiny. The hope of being reunited with loved ones and friends is very meaningful to senior adults.

Albert L. Cardwell shares a similar story of how an aging widow adjusts to the loss of her husband. It may help some senior adult who struggles to adjust to life alone.

Alma and Clarence were married when he was seventeen and she fifteen. The young husband was a farmer, and his wife often went into the fields to work with him. Soon a succession of children occupied most of her time. Of the twelve who were born, nine survived to adulthood.

As farming in North Georgia became a more difficult livelihood, Clarence began work in a clothing plant during the week, doing his farm work in the afternoons and on weekends. Later, as the demands of a large family became greater, he opened a shoe repair shop on Saturdays, for a total of three jobs.

In time the last of the children were grown and married. Each one left the little village to find employment elsewhere, leaving the aging couple alone. Back trouble forced Clarence to retire, and they spent a few years in the empty nest. He died from a heart attack, leaving Alma alone.

She became deaf and had to use a special telephone, even with her hearing aid. Clarence had always done the driving, handled the money, and made the decisions; now Alma could not drive or write a check, and scarcely knew how to shop for groceries. Not only did she have to work through her grief at his death, but she faced a reorganization of her whole pattern of living. She had no close neighbors and was terrified by the thought of living alone. Sixty-six years old, Alma faced the prospect of being alone and deaf, unable to hear should an intruder try to force entry.

She visited her children, trying to delay the time when she would be alone at home. But she soon found that nothing could take the place of her own home. She mastered the fundamentals of paying the bills, opened a bank account, and began to make her own decisions. Transportation was a problem, but gradually she made the necessary adjustment.[29]

Recently, for some reason, my wife and I were discussing death. I reminded her that marriages as we have known them would not exist in the life beyond. Silently, she turned to walk away. I saw that her eyes were filled with tears as she turned again to face me. Softly, but yet with determination, she spoke, "Well, you are going to be my best friend."

No philosophy or psychology, except one that is Christian, can describe the faith, hope, and love which flow from the fact of endless tomorrows in Christ.

### Facing dying and death

Elizabeth Kubler-Ross has reminded us of the trauma that may be experienced as one faces his own death. The loss of significant others by death or other forms of separation is traumatic, but when one dies he is separated from all. She said,

> The patient should not be encouraged to look at the sunny side of things, as this would mean he should not contemplate his impending death. It would be contraindicated to tell him not to be sad, since all of us are tremendously sad when we lose one beloved person. The patient is in the process of losing everything and everybody he loves.[30]

As already discussed, research indicates that most senior adults are not fearful of death. Dying is another subject and that is why Kubler-Ross titled her book, *On Death and Dying.* An awareness of death, a distinctive soul function, has persisted throughout life since the early years of childhood. In general, senior adults have accepted this final stage of life. Yet, the moment of truth, the actual experience of dying is rarely free from anxieties about loved ones, suffering, indignities, and life beyond. However, there is consolation that one is moving toward the completion of a circle. Although dying is personal, it is not an unparalleled event. Many others have gone through this door before us. One is walking down a well-worn path.[31] Some senior adults are not rushing death but valuing it.

A 93-year-old man beamed affirmatively when one of the writers commented. "I think you like talking about your death because . . . well, your death is something you *have.*" "It's mine," the elder rejoined. "Don't belong to nobody else."[32]

Regardless of the positive experimental results about the death fears of senior adults, death and dying must be faced and seen in Christian perspective. The closeness of death for an elderly population in general is a distinctive. None of us is certain of earthly life beyond this moment, but the older person is less certain, and rightly so. He needs to admit that death is closer for him than the average person in other age groups. Jerome Ellison in his book, *The Last Third of Life Club,* placed emphasis on the word *admit*—I admit that death is closer for me than the average person and in this respect I am different.[33]

Since ageism obviously flourishes in the Western world, an analysis of one related cause may be in order. Age and death must be almost synonymous to the human mind. If one accepts his age he must, of necessity, accept his nearness to death. This has a positive ring. However, the best defense of age may be an acceptance of death in a defiant act—a rebellion against a youth or middle-age oriented society. If such defiance has shewed the experimental studies, then facing death is a more serious problem in the lives of senior adults than we have been led to believe.

## Facing ageism

One of the tasks of senior adults is facing ageism. First, a definition is needed to arrive at a common meaning as we consider this recent attitude. A brief account of important social structures and change may help to understand the etiology of elements of ageism from a broad perspective. A brief review of several myths is described with no attempts at presenting the possible dynamics for their perpetuation. A psychological study of the dynamics of myths about senior adults is needed. It would help destroy their roots. Last, the responsibility of senior adults to ageism deserves mention.

## Definition of "ageism"

Robert N. Butler states that the stereotyping and myths surrounding old age can be explained partly by ignorance of senior adults and a lack of contact with a wide variety of older people. However, he sees " . . . another powerful factor operating—a deep and profound prejudice against the elderly which is found to some degree in all of us."[34] Butler coined the word in 1968. He defined *ageism* as "discrimination directed by one age group against another." As such, he saw it similar in impact to other and more familiar forms of bigotry—sexism and racism.[35] Ageism is seen in many forms and in many places. Stereotypes and myths, dislike and disdain, avoidance, cartoons, epithets, jokes, and discriminatory practices are expressions of this pervasive prejudice. Butler said:

At times ageism becomes an expedient method by which society promotes viewpoints about the aged in order to relieve itself of responsibility toward them. At other times ageism serves a highly personal objective, protecting younger (usually middle-aged) individuals—often at high emotional cost—from thinking about things they fear (aging, illness, death).[36]

*Social change and ageism*

Ewald W. Busse has reported on theories on the valuing of senior adults as they are related to social structure and change. Three theories are:

1. Senior adults are valued more in a static society than they are in one where rapid change is taking place;

2. Senior adults are valued more when they are fewer in number in a population than when they are more numerous;

3. Senior adults are valued more in a society where they are able to perform useful and socially valued functions.[37]

Two of these three theories offer a doubtful future for senior adults because their numbers are increasing in a chaotic and changing society. However, when Busse reported on the third theory, mandatory retirement was still in effect. With the present laws, more and more senior adults may provide useful and valued functions in the labor market. However, senior adults may not continue to be employed, but this possibility does not exclude them from finding and performing socially valued roles. Possibly their choice to find useful roles outside the labor market may be more acceptable as they become an increasingly larger group. This would make room for successive generations.

## Myths

All social scientists are hurrying about to discover the truth about aging to counter the illusions, delusions, and stereotypes concocted back in 1900 that do not fit reality. With 90 percent of senior adults vital, involved, and independent thinkers we must work fast to dispel myths. We must make use of all this potential.[38]

*The myth of sexual impotence.* In the minds of many, sex is for youth and not age. When connected with senior adults it is tied very closely to a thought such as "dirty old man!" Psychologists and marriage counselors have shown that sex is mainly psychological. Thus, physical aging may be determinative to a limited degree for a decline in sexual potency. This is true because over two-thirds of senior adults are afflicted with one or more chronic physical problems. Some of the physical factors that may adversely affect sexual functioning are as follows:

1. Medication for hypertension and other disorders. Some medications are notorious for lessinging the sexual drive

2. Skeletal and muscular disorders of the back. A condition called osteoporosis, a softening of the bones, may develop

3. Infection and other disorders of the prostate gland

4. Inadequate diet —

There are some who believe that certain degenerative changes which attack most forcibly at the time of middle age and beyond could be prevented at least partially by a proper diet that would include natural foods and food supplements. Vitamin E and the food elements contained in wheat germ have been shown to be extremely important for the sexual health of farm animals.

. . . . . . . . . . . . . . . . . . . . . . . . . . . . . . . . . . . . . . . . . . . . . . . . . . . . . . . . . . . . . . . . . . .

A report from a medical magazine has shown that patients after given vitamins A and E together restored the normal number of sperm cells.[39]

5. Thyroid disturbances.

A simple listing of pertinent facts about sex for senior adults may be helpful.

1. Taboos against sex in old age have interfered with in-depth investigations of sex for the senior adult.

2. Because of the taboos about sex and age, investigators have not been comfortable in investigating sex and the senior adult.

3. Eric Pfeiffer maintains that the current taboo is more than a carry-over from the Victorian Age. "Our society still holds that sexual activity should be engaged in primarily for procreative, only secondarily for recreative purposes."[40]

4. Many people believe that sexual desire and activity ceases when one becomes a senior adult.[41]

5. Outstanding sex researchers find a waning of sexual response among senior adults. This decline may not be due to aging.

6. Prominent sex researchers suggest that most senior adults are active sexually if they were active when young. Disease and other factors may thwart this sexuality altogether or be the cause of some decline.

7. Just as physiological factors are important in senior-adult sexuality so are psychological factors. Depression interupts sexual activity.

8. Male senior adults maintain an interest in sex but wane in sexual activity.

9. Female senior adults have much less interest in sex and are much less active. Sex may be painful for females, or fewer outlets are available.

10. Most male senior adults reported strong sexual feelings in their younger years while only a third of the women in the sample reported comparable sexual feelings in their youth.[42]

The belief that sex and senior adults are not compatible is a myth. Most studies included older persons who were sexually active into the latter years.

*Myths about senility.* Senility has been identified with old age. It is not considered to be an inevitable concomitant of old age but is a predictable and curable disorder. The word "senility" is losing favor in the jargon of psychologists, psychiatrists, and general practitioners. One teacher of note has stated that senility is not a physical (organic) problem, but is emotional. It is a form of psychosis, or break with reality.

Approximately ten years ago psychologists from the University of Michigan came forth with data that indicated that the condition of three fourths of those committed to nursing homes could have been reversed. Of course, the physical and psychological conditions, when allowed to continue, make the condition almost irreversible and the problem becomes chronic.

Little doutbt exists that some impairment of brain tissue function may be present in what is called senility. However, anxiety, depression, grief, and a full range of psychological problems afflict senior adults as well as all age groups. It is very easy to blame old age and brain damage as culprits and literally give up. Too many examples of reversals are seen to be so fatalistic about periods of confusion in senior adults. Even the deterioration of brain cells may be halted to some degree. In the instances when there is organic brain damage, what has been unfortunately called "senility" does exist. However, just as in any other physical illness there are numerous psychological overtones which respond to loving care.[43] Actual impairment of brain tissue function will be discussed in chapter 5.

*Myth of serenity.* Again, the problem of maintaining a realistic and balanced perspective of senior adults haunts them and us. To visualize them as gentle, soft-spoken, garden tenders and cookie bakers is extremely limited. Such stereotypes distort reality to the point that the problems of senior adults are ignored. Television and advertising, in general, complicate matters with their rocking chair scenes. Possibly, that which fosters such distortions is called a "denial mechanism" the weakest form of defense. The human mind is marvelously equipped at escaping unpleasant situations. It would be bad psychology to cause a consumer to identify a product with a suffering parent.

*The myth of chronological aging.* Ideas about aging as being chronological are a myth. All too often the passing of the years is considered synonymous with growing old. I have already written briefly about psychological time. Time has never aged anyone. Aging is a development that occurs within our understanding of chronological time. In spite of this myth it apparently has been necessary to set a chronological year for the beginning of senior adulthood. Butler has declared chronological age as " . . . a convenient but imprecise indicator of physical, mental, and emotional status."[44]

*The myth of unproductivity.* Figures in chapter 1 on the employment of senior adults should dispel this myth to some degree. In 1975 approximately one-third of men sixty-five to sixty-nine years of age were participating in the labor force. Only 14 percent of women in the same age group were employed. If these figures are not substantial enough to convince the general public of older Americans' involvement or desire for participation in the labor market, other realities should. How is it possible to register greater involvement in the face of mandatory retirement? General observations reveal a strong political, religious, and general volunteer involvement.

## Development (Adjustment and Beyond)

Brief mention has been made of a distinction between adjustment and development. In reality, the manner in which a senior adult adjusts to the loss of a spouse determines, at least, a significant part of the development of that person. Parallel to this supreme loss may be other changes and choices related to the process of development occurring at the same time. To limit a senior adult's growth or development to his adaptation to all forms of internal and external forces is to see him only as reacting to life. It may be argued that most of life is reacting, adjusting, or adapting to change. Certainly, much of life is responding to influences, attraction, and interaction, but there is a transcendence about a living soul that initiates without being caused to initiate. Some of our greatest theologians have recognized the problem of succumbing only to a "cause and effect" explanation of our universe. For this reason, I must make a large place for the senior adult's "just choosing to be." This creative potential in man is Godlike and defies the modern scientific notions of the physical sciences. We have fallen before the very obvious evidences of the cause and effect sequences that literally fill our lives. There is room for determinism in the physical world and in the lives of human beings, mainly because they are lifeless, dead in trespasses and sin, and tossed to and fro. The predictability of the "cause and effect" physical world gives us cause for reassurance as we crank our cars, send men to the moon, and depend so heavily upon medical and industrial technology.

I am not subscribing to a deadly dualism that makes the physical world and the mental and spiritual world arch enemies. I am saying that a living soul is different than a rock and that he/she does have some choice in how he/she adjusts to change. Also, persons may choose without being caused to choose and, hopefully, this is in the direction of becoming the best that their creative minds can visualize. As you can determine through reading these opening statements, I intend to be loyal to those who have outlined theories for successful aging which may be adjustment in nature. They offer exceptional insights. Also, the reader needs to briefly review Havighurst's outline and James A. Thorson's additional learning tasks.

## Aging as development

The life span seen from a biological perspective has been a Western view. Life is viewed as physical growth, a plateau of maintenance, and then, deterioration. This is not all of the picture. The developmental theories of personality as reflected in general and Christian psychology provide us with a more complete account. The concept "development" is neither positive nor negative in the use that we have for it. The concept is large enough to allow for positive physical growth or deterioration. Also, mental, social, and spiritual dimensions may be subsumed under the idea of development that allows for both positive and negative growth. Even biological deterioration, from a Christian perspective, may portend of positive development as physical decline makes way for the development of more durable qualities of life and prepares the ground for the flowering plants of a new world.

## Popular theories of successful aging

In part 1 of the excellent book, *Aging in America,* edited by Kart and Manard, an outstanding symposium of theories of social aging by noted authors is presented. Five theories are presented which are related to the adjustment and development of senior adults. Although society is the setting from which the theories are abstracted, ultimately, the self-concepts and life satisfactions that are derived from these social happenings are psychological. Again, much of the manner in which an individual sees himself is determined by his social relationships or, at least, provides the opportunity for seeing himself in varying ways. The reader can see how constantly we must train to do battle with ideas that make man largely the victim of society. Only two of the theories, the disengagement theory and the activity theory will be extracted from the five suggested. A third theory of development, not presented by Kart and Manard, is added.

## Theory of disengagement

At first glance, the theory of disengagement is viewed with suspicion. It suggests withdrawal and to many this means "retreat," "looseness," "a breach," "quitting," and so on. Maybe disengagement was an unfortunate choice of a word by Elaine Cumming and W. Henry to describe the "mutual withdrawal between the aging individual and others in the social system to which he belongs."[45] The main argument for the theory is that if Mr. Jacobson gradually withdraws from society and society gradually withdraws from him, then both will be better off than were a sudden, traumatic separation to be the results of a lack of disengagement.

## Activity theory

This theory is the most popular theory of successful aging. It fits the work ethic of our nation. Thus, the psychological implications of inactivity may be substantial. Those who hold to this theory maintain that the senior adults who age successfully resist the aging and fight to stay young. In order to stop the economic, social, physical, psychological, and spiritual decline, the senior adult should maintain the activities of middle age as long as possible. A value judgment is made at this point that it is better to be active than inactive. Obviously, many senior adults cannot or will not attempt to maintain a middle-age style of life. Large numbers manage to do this successfully.[46]

I subscribe to much of the truth of the activity theory. However, when inevitable, limited activity arrives, what then? Is it really true that one must be active to age successfully? There must be some theory that combines the truth and reality of disengagement and the sterling values of appropriate activity.

## Developmental theory

The developmental theory is built on the idea of a life cycle which emphasizes an individual life-style. The theory, also called continuity theory, " . . . attempts to explain what is apparent to even a casual observer of older people—that both busy older people and disengaged older people can be happy or unhappy, depending on forces more mysterious, or at least less evident, than the simple level of activity in their lives."[47]

This attractive theory has implications for a Christian psychology. As the individual develops some options are closed, others open, and a variety of creative choices are available. These may be presented by the circumstances of life (providence of God, also), or by the transcendent qualities of a living soul. Thus, life can be seen as activity, disengagement, choice, rejection, as one moves upward or deep. Often, soul growth has been described as a movement into the depths of life. Rather than biological deterioration being the order of the day, aging can be growth toward God.

Marcia J. Cameron pointed out that the findings relative to the developmental theory of aging "suggest that a spiritual dimension to aging is something more than a pious hope, something which happens only to a few wise men."[48]

## Other theories

Three other theories of note are (1) role theory, (2) subculture theory, and (3) age stratification theory. Role theory proponents maintain that successful aging has to do with the giving up of roles typical of adulthood and the acceptance of roles prescribed for the later years. The subculture theory, although vitally related to other theories, has a distinctive element which sees senior adults as members of a subculture. Identification with and self-suffering within this culture may provide the possibility of successful aging. The age stratification theory is a proposal by Matilda White Riley for understanding senior adults as they are seen as one ingredient, "inseparable and interdependent with the other age strata."[49]

*Havighurst's proposed adjustment tasks*

Over thirty years ago Robert J. Havighurst proposed six developmental or adjustment tasks for senior adults. Much of our thinking in the last three decades about growing older has focused on these six tasks. The adjustment tasks already discussed in some detail include several of those proposed by Havighurst. Briefly listed, they are:

1. Adjusting to decreasing physical strength and health
2. Adjusting to retirement and reduced income
3. Adjusting to death of a spouse
4. Establishing an explicit affiliation with one's age group
5. Adopting and adapting social roles in a flexible way
6. Establishing satisfactory physical living arrangements[50]

James A. Thorson commented on Havighurst's concerns relative to particular decades of life that govern a person's behavior. Thorson suggested additional learning tasks for senior adults in the years to come while noting Havighurst's emphases on the tasks of "deciding whether to disengage and how" and "making the most of disengagement," for the decades of the sixties and the seventies, respectively. Thorson added the following tasks which are related but move beyond adaptation into a more self-initiated stance:

1. Adapting to change
2. Continuing to grow
3. Perpetuating the culture
4. Putting one's life into perspective
5. Finding self-acceptance[51]

At this point, it is interesting to note that not all senior adults major on disengagement—a mutual withdrawal of the senior adult and society. Longitudinal studies have shown little evidence to support the theory that successful aging is the result of this mutual withdrawal.[52]

*Motivation and personality development*

The description of drives, originally termed "instincts," is a highly debatable matter in psychology. Sex, hunger, thirst, curiosity, intracranial stimulation, and so forth, are usually considered as drives arising from internal imbalances. In other words, drives are the result of needs. Behavior is caused by drives, and changes in behavior occur as the result of needs being met.

Other drives toward aggression, approval, and achievement are seen by many modern psychologists as being developed because of the expectations of society. These may be seen as arising from external imbalances. Thus, many present-day psychologists see motivation as a combination of needs, drives, behavior, and satisfaction.

Much of this sequence fits into the cause-effect explanation that is so beneficial in the physiological sciences but needs clarification for a psychology of soul. Of course, there is much truth in the sequence because senior adults are physical and social beings. And, the need for God has been claimed as a fundamental need in human personality by many theologians for years. Thus, the need, drive, behavior, and satisfaction sequence does not damage the idea that man is incurably religious and can only be satisfied as he finds his peace in a proper relationship to God.

A most helpful tool in understanding the development of personality has been theorized by Salvatore R. Maddi, author of *Personality Theories: A Comparative Analysis.* His theory may help us make some order out of the conglomeration of ideas about how senior adults develop.

The first emphasis in this chapter has been on the process of development as senior adults adjust to changes and crises in their lives. The same process of adjustment should be a part of all theories of development because meeting the tasks, changes, and crises of life are real! However, there is more. Thus, one purpose of this section will be to strengthen a personal view that personality development can be more than adjustment.

Maddi takes many theories of personality and places them under three models. He titles them the conflict model, fulfillment model, and consistency model.[53]

*Conflict model*

In this model it is theorized that a person is in a bind between opposing forces. There is a clash and the best the individual can do is to arrive at some compromise between these forces. These forces are thought of as being between the individual and society, and, as life versus death forces within the individual. It is easy to see this battle as similar to the personal struggle Paul the apostle, described in Romans 7:15-25. Little doubt exists that such conflicts do shape personality, but for Freud, Erikson, and many others this struggle is the key to how personality develops. For any theory of personality to be acceptable it must have a core tendency that is present in all human beings. Thus, it is a universal tendency at the heart of human nature. *The core tendency in the conflict model is* "to reduce tension and anxiety as much as possible by minimizing conflict.[54] The development of some senior adults may be seen as avoiding a compromise between themselves and society and they do what they want to do, where, and when. Others give up all individuality and become compliant and thus, only react or adapt to society's expectations. Within the framework of this theory one can see the inner conflict that is present when the force of life draws one to keep moving forward to participate in life. At the same time, another force is pushing toward disengagement or withdrawal wherein there is a fear of death. Each of us feels this tension between life and death within us. To illustrate, I have a dear friend in his sixties who could easily win a prominent political office if he were to make a bid for it. A real ambivalence exists when he considers the difficulties and anxieties of the job were he to win and the lost opportunities which could result were he to not run for the office.

What I am attempting to say is that the conflict model does help us see one possible explanation of the struggle and conflicts that besiege senior adults. I am not saying that *all* personality development is the result of conflict.

### Fulfillment model

Whereas the conflict model explanation of personality development includes opposing forces, the fulfillment model assumes only one great force of living. Conflict gets in the way of the one great force but conflict is not inevitable or basic. The basic premise of this theory is that life is the unfolding of the one great force. The conflict model views development more as an animalistic survival. Of course, we struggle with a nature that is self-centered and characterized by compromise. However, the fulfillment model places an emphasis upon the human and the realization of his inherent capabilities. You will recognize in this statement the influence of Carl R. Rogers and Abraham Maslow.

Alfred Adler, Henry White, Gordon Allport, Erich Fromm, and others stress the perfection of life through reaching out for ideals.[55] This has been named the "perfection version" and approaches something of the meaning we find in Scripture.

The fulfillment model with self-actualization, personal development, and the perfection of life has captured the imagination of modern America. Personal growth is not anti-Christian nor is the striving for perfection (or love). However, if personal growth is the senior adult's supreme goal, or, he thinks that it is achieved by his own doing, then these are non-Christian.

*Consistency model*

This model does not stress forces, inherited or otherwise. The emphasis is upon an internal consistency, that is to say, "Are my concepts about God consistent?" or "Are my perceptions of God consistent?" Another way of clarifying this model is to say that people are anxious when they have incompatibilities in their thinking and therefore their lives evolve out of the struggle to achieve consistency in thoughts.[56]

Lucien E. Coleman in his book, *Understanding Adults,* discusses the cognitive-dissonance version of the consistency model in his explanations on why it is difficult for some adults to undertake new learning tasks. New ideas, new observations, and contrary beliefs require anxiety and energy to maintain the harmony of thinking that is desirable.[57]

Another facet of the consistency model has to do, in the main, with emotions. Unless the tensions and emotions that an individual experiences are consistent with the customary level of excitation then all behavior is an attempt to overcome this inconsistency.[58]

*A Christian model*

As you can see, the various models which serve as convenient categories for many theories of development are informative. The struggle with conflicts, the desire for fulfillment, and to have peace of mind and wholeness are really not alien to our Christian faith. They really are pictures of the condition of man without God and many times even with God. A simple core tendency may be isolated for all human nature as we are informed by this psychology and our Christian theology. At first, all men must say, "I must give myself to me and satisfy me." Later, though by acculturation the individual learns a prudential ethic that protects him by protecting others. This is better than before. Again, he may lose himself in Christ and thus find himself. This is no sacrifice of identity and personhood, it is the finding of oneself. The one great force is God who from nothing made the world and us! Thus, conflicts, fulfillment, integrity of thought, and peace may be ours through faith in Christ. The freedom to become as we ought to become can only be found in him! In Christ, ye shall be free indeed.[59] The core tendency then must be, "For to me to live is Christ."[60]

I may have overtaxed you with this discussion of motivation. However, the deepest motives within senior adults send them running in particular directions. The basic motive for most possibly will not be to lift up Christ. However, a meaning for life that is larger than oneself is essential in facing conflicts, realizing one's full potential, and the fearless search for wholeness and truth. This meaning can be found in Christ!

## Uphill and downhill development

The eight steps toward maturity as presented in the writings of Erik Erikson[61] allow only one developmental stage for senior adults. The stage is termed "integrity versus despair."

The first stage according to Erikson is the stage of trust *versus* mistrust which spans the initial fifteen months of life. It is during this brief time that the ability to trust others, self, and the environment may develop as opposed to the growth of a general distrust. What an important developmental period this is for the rest of life, especially in the eventual directing of this trust toward God. The development of trust is determined by the amount of conflict and trauma experienced by the infant.

The second stage is autonomy *versus* shame and doubt and encompasses the first thirty-six months of life. The development of the positive potentials in this period are built on trust and are a necessary foundation for later independence.

The third stage, initiative *versus* guilt, covers the fourth and fifth years of life. This ability to initiate life rather than react to life is essential for future choices that are the person's as opposed to compliance to others' decisions. Senior adults may be almost equally divided into two groups. One group is defense-oriented—persons who react to defend themselves. The other group is task-oriented people—persons who initiate actions because they consider them necessary to complete important and desirable tasks.

The fourth stage, industry *versus* inferiority, flows through years six through eleven. The importance of a sense of accomplishment throughout life is obvious. Self-esteem has been considered superior to intelligence for achievement in most fields of endeavor.

The fifth stage, identity *versus* role diffusion, describes an adolescent development task. The dramatic changes from childhood toward adulthood present a crucial task for the individual as he attempts to discover his personal identity. This search is lifelong but is intensified in adolescence.

The sixth stage, intimacy versus isolation, is that period when one needs to be close to someone else in a comprehensive manner. If trust, initiative, identity, and the other positive poles have not been reached it is difficult to get close enough to share in intimacy.

The seventh stage, generativity *versus* stagnation, occurs in adulthood. The positive pole has been termed the "parental sense." The growth expected for this stage is the ability to look beyond oneself to the next generation. It means foregoing one's own comfort and concern in favor of helping our children and preparing for future generations.

The eighth stage, ego integrity *versus* despair, encompasses a large number of years from middle-age until death. The positive pole is the wholeness and completeness that is experienced as one comes to peace with himself and society.

A brief review of these hardwon plateaus of development is necessary if we are to see the ever-present prospects of decline and regression that threaten senior adults. If a realistic appraisal of development, positive and negative, is presented then I must present honestly the negative potentiality for senior adults.

Briefly, let us revere the process theorized by Erik Erikson. Imagine that as a result of inadequate supports and advocacy a senior adult despairs. He may become threatened by survival and great needs until his constant preoccupation is with himself. No concern exists for others and much less for future generations. Withdrawal is necessitated because there is no desire for sharing—there is fear of sharing or it becomes only a one-way sharing—complaints. The physiological changes are more dramatic than in adolescence and the shallow or unknown roles of senior adults are diffused, confused, and deserted. The destructive loss of identity adds to the desire for withdrawal and complicates the process of industry and accomplishment. Little strength and confidence is left for initiative and next an almost complete dependency descends. Last, with relationship ties abandoned and self enthroned in the center of a threatening world, mistrust slowly creeps into every corner of life. Each sound in the night is a thief. Windows and doors are nailed shut and a threatened infant seeks the peace of a mother's womb.

This is a sad picture that hopefully is rarely seen. I have learned that no one is ever completely secure in life. We are reminded to take heed lest we fall. Senior adults and those who care should maintain constant vigilance in not only maintaining the levels of development but pressing forward to even greater heights. Someone has said that to hesitate at one point in a mountain climb brings about a preoccupation with balance. It is better to move on, cautiously, but ever higher.

Erik Erikson improved upon the works of Freud by giving us eight psychosocial stages that demonstrate the importance of family relationships. He moved beyond a biological and sexual explanation for personality growth. John J. Gleason, Jr., in *Growing Up to God* has used Erikson's stages to show how an understanding of God may be achieved as one moves through the stages of growth.[62]

The psychological functions are really soul functions when seen in relationship to God. The development of trust or faith has obvious theological implications. The developing of initiative is vitally related to the development of conscience. Each successive stage is dependent on the former stage and all the while the trust is growing as one is autonomous, initiates, and so forth. Caring and love are expressed in intimacy and generativity. Thus, the growth of the functions essential to relate to a living God begin in early family relationships. Faith, love, conscience, awareness of death are capacities that must be developed first in early relationships and then perfected in relationship to Christ.

## Development of characteristic tendencies

Robert N. Butler has given us ten characteristics which are presented as tendencies that occur in the lives of most senior adults. "They are not inevitable nor are they found in the same degree in each person who manifests them."[63] They are:

1. A change in the sense of time—Time is viewed differently by the senior adult. Future, past, present, and the passing of time are seen differently in the latter years.

2. A sense of the entire life cycle—Senior adults may see the entire span of life from the vantage point of one who is nearing the completion of the circle.

3. A tendency toward life review—Senior adults have a tendency to look back over their lives and review past experiences.

4. A tendency to try to overcome guilt—Senior adults are constantly attempting to make restitution for things for which they have guilt.

5. An attachment to the familiar—Senior adults usually are very attached to familiar objects which surround them.

6. Conservation of continuity—Senior adults desire to pass on to the next generation skills, counsel, and so on, which they have considered worthwhile to them.

7. A desire to leave a legacy—Senior adults want to leave something of themselves behind when they die.

8. Transmission of power—Many senior adults will arrive at a time in their lives, if they live long enough, when they will give to one or several significant persons their power and authority.

9. A sense of fulfillment of life—A large number of senior adults will

experience a sense of satisfaction about life.

10. Capacity for growth—The later years may be the doorways into unbelievable growth which many senior adults will enter.[64]

*Potential for the development of life's greatest values*

It is appropriate that the last of Butler's ten characteristics has to do with a capacity for growth. Most theories of personality development have been described with a particular developmental stage achieved every few years in young life. An example, already examined, is seen in the writings of Erikson. Trust, autonomy, initiative, and a sense of industry—four different stages of growth—may develop in the first seven to ten years of life. Only one level of maturity, ego integrity versus despair, is assigned by Erikson for as much as thirty to fifty years of middle and old age.[65] Very little attention has been given to the possibility that life's most desirable characteristics, traits, values, and other levels of maturity are developed in these years of great potentiality. The potential beauty of old age has been ignored in large measure.

There exists in man a gift of God's grace which is the capacity for change and decision. Christians and non-Christians have this ability which can be exercised freely in Christ. Thus, man can choose to become, not only through environmental stress but because of free will to actualize those Christlike attributes that are the most prized and needed in our society. A noted personologist-psychologist arbitrarily chose sixty years of age as the minimum time in which a person could realize his greatest potential. It is doubtful if he could have been accurate in this precise line of demarcation, but I tend to agree with him and respect his very positive views of life and his choice of experimental subjects who were men of religion.

Robert Peck has given us three beautiful stages of growth which may occur in the lives of senior adults. They are as follows:

1. Ego differentiation *versus* work-role preoccupation
2. Body transcendance *versus* body preoccupation
3. Self-transcendance *versus* self-preoccupation[66]

Within these stages of growth the author has made room for God! Yes, with him the sunset may be more beautiful than the sunrise, and the first part of life be fulfilled in the last. When one walks with God the horizon is limitless.

## NOTES

[1]Otto Pollack, *Social Adjustment in Old Age: A Research Planning Report*, Social Science Research Council Bulletin No. 59 (New York: Social Science Research Council, 1948), p. 33.

[2]Ruth S. Cavan, Ernest W. Burgess, Robert J. Havighurst, and Herbert Goldhamer, *Personal Adjustment in Old Age* (Chicago: Science Research Associates, 1949), p. 15.

[3]James A. Thorson, *Psychology of Aging*, Unit 2 in the series of monographs: Profiles of Aging—Gerontology Readings for Health Professions (Omaha, Neb.: University of Nebraska Medical Center, 1978), p. 52.

[4]Martin E. Seligman, *Helplessness—On Repression, Development, and Death* (San Francisco: W. H. Freeman Co., 1975), p. 86.

[5]Avery Weisman, *On Dying and Denying: A Psychiatric Study of Terminality* (New York: Behavioral Publications, Inc., 1972), p. 161.

[6]Hans Selye, *Stress Without Distress*, 9th ed. (New York: Signet, 1974), p. 17.

[7]Tim LaHaye, *How to Win Over Depression* (Grand Rapids, Mich.: Zondervan, 1974), p. 21.

[8]Thomas W. Klewin, "Coping with Life Changes and Family Stress," *Home Life*, 30 (March 1976) 28.

[9]Hans Selye, *Stress without Distress*, pp. 18-20.

[10]Ibid., p. 35.

[11]Judith G. Rabkin and Elmer L. Struening, "Life Events, Stress, Illness," *Science*, 194 (December 3, 1976) p. 1014.

[12]Rabkin and Strueing, "Life Events, Stress, and Illness," p. 1018.

[13]LaHaye, *How to Win Over Depression*, p. 101.

[14]E. L. Bartz, *Creative Aging* (New York: The Macmillan Co., 1963), p. 155.

[15]James A. Thorson, *Psychology of Aging*, p. 44.

[16]Ibid., pp. 44-45.

[17]Oates, *Christ and Selfhood*, p. 147.

[18]Harold L. Sheppard, "The Potential Role of Behavioral Science in the Solution of the 'Older Worker Problem,' " p. 74.

[19]Ibid.

[20]From *The Gift of Retirement* by Liliane Giudice © John Knox Press. Used by permission of the publisher.

[21]Anonymous.

[22]Daniel J. Levinson, *The Seasons of a Man's Life* (New York: Alfred A. Knopf, Inc., 1978), p. 35.

[23]Ibid., pp. 35-36.

[24]Robert N. Butler, *Why Survive?* p. 416.

[25]T. B. Maston, "Adjustments in Mature Years," *Home Life* (July 1974), p. 48.

[26]Robert Kastenbaum and Sandra E. Candy, "The 4% Fallacy: A Methodological and Empirical Critique of Extended Care Facility Population Statistics," in *Aging in America*, eds. Gary S. Kart and Barbara B. Manard (Port Washington, N.Y.: Alfred Publishing Co., Inc., 1976), p. 167.

[27]T. B. Maston, "Adjustments in the Mature Years," p. 48.

[28]1 Corinthians 15:17.

[29]Albert L. Cardwell, *Life Alone: The World of the Formerly Married* (Nashville: The Sunday School Board of the Southern Baptist Convention, 1976), p. 21.

[30]Elizabeth Kubler-Ross, *On Death and Dying* (New York: The Macmillan Publishing Co., Inc., 1969), 1969), p. 87.

[31]Kastenbaum and Aisenberg, *The Psychology of Death*, p. 105.

[32]Ibid.

[33]Jerome Ellison, *The Last Third of Life Club* (Philadelphia: A Pilgrim Press Book, 1973), pp. 11-13.

[34]Butler, *Why Survive?* p. 11.

[35]Robert N. Butler, "Age-ism: Another Form of Bigotry," *Gerontologist*, 1969, 9:243-46.

[36]Butler, *Why Survive?* p. 12.

[37]Ewald W. Busse, "Theories of Aging," in *Behavior and Adaptation in Late Life*, eds. Ewald W. Busse and Eric Pfeiffer (Boston: Little, Brown and Company, 1969), pp. 24-25.

[38]*Your Retirement Psychology Guide*, American Association of Retired Persons and National Retired Teachers Association, Long Beach, Ca., 1973.

[39]Harold C. Steele and Charles B. Crow, *How to Deal with Aging and the Elderly* (Huntsville, Ala.: The Strode Publishers, 1970), p. 41.

[40]Eric Pfeiffer, "Sexual Behavior in Old Age," in *Behavior and Adaptation in Late Life*, eds. Ewald W. Busse and Eric Pfeiffer (Boston: Little, Brown and Co., 1969), p. 131.

[41]Ibid.

[42]E. Pfeiffer, A Verwoerdt, and H. S. Wang, "The Natural History of Sexual Behavior in a Biologically Advantaged Group of Aged Individuals," *Journal of Gerontology*, 1969, 24:193.

[43]Butler, *Why Survive?* pp. 9-10.

[44]Ibid., p. 7.

[45]Kart and Manard, *Aging in America*, p. 4.

[46]Marcia J. Cameron, *Views of Aging, A Teachers' Guide* (Ann Arbor, Mich.: Institute of Gerontology, The University of Michigan-Wayne State University, 1976), p. 141.

[47]Ibid., p. 142.

[48]Ibid.

[49]Kart and Manard, eds, *Aging in America*, pp. 3-5.

[50]Robert J. Havighurst, *Developmental Tasks and Education* (New York: David McKay Co., 1974), pp. 108-16.

[51]James A. Thorson, "Future Trends in Education for Older Adults," in *An Introduction to Educational Gerontology*, vol. 1. eds. Ronald Sherron and Barry Lumsden (Washington, D.C.: Hemisphere Publishing Corp., 1976), pp. 203-27.

[52]Busse, "Theories of Aging," pp. 27-28.

[53]Salvatore R. Maddi, *Personality Theories: A Comparative Analysis*, 3rd ed. (Homewood, Ill.: The Dorsey Press, 1976), pp. 19-21.

[54]Ibid. p. 176.

[55]Ibid., p. 179.

[56]Ibid., pp. 181-82.

[57]Lucien E. Coleman, Jr., *Understanding Adults* (Nashville: Convention Press, 1969), pp. 130-133.

[58]Maddi, *Personality Theories*, p. 182.

[59]John 8:36.

[60]Philippians 1:21.

[61]Erik H. Erikson, *Childhood and Society* (New York: W. W. Norton & Co., 1950), pp. 221-32.

[62]John J. Gleason, Jr., *Growing Up to God* (Nashville: Abingdon Press, 1975), p. 21.

[63]Butler, *Why Survive?* p. 409.

[64]Ibid., pp. 409-17.

[65]Erikson, *Childhood and Society*, pp. 221-32.

[66]Robert Peck, "Psychological Developments in the Second Half of Life," in *Human Life Cycle,* ed. William C. Sze (New York: Jason Aronson, Inc., 1975), pp. 615-17.

# 6

# Psychological Disorders

*Questions?*

When one begins to talk about psychological problems the first question is, "What caused that problem?" It appears to be a reflex action of defense that usually comes before the problem is described. For years, I have attempted to teach students to recognize the different psychological disorders, attempt to understand the person better, help through prevention or counseling, and to refer the person, if needed. Thus, let me warn the reader, through experience with my students, about trying to understand senior adults by understanding some of the disorders presented in this chapter. First, you will want to know, "What caused the problem?" Secondly, you will think, "I believe I have that problem."

*Side effects*

You may get very upset and sometimes sick over the idea that you are trying to understand something that frightens you and appears to be beyond your control and, for that matter, anybody's control.

One outstanding doctoral student came for clinical training at a mental hospital where I was the supervisor for clinical pastoral training. He had great difficulty getting through the day without having a bad headache. However, he was only one of many who came and suffered for the experiences of studying psychological disorders.

The word *iatrogeny* has, in the main, been used to describe the side effects of medication. Yes, sometimes the treatment is more devastating than the problem! Someone has said, "Our solutions are our main problems." This is too true for humor. The side effects of medication may sometimes outweigh its benefits. The word *iatrogeny* has also been used to describe the side effects of other types of treatment which hinges on diagnosis. As a result of the study of problems, we imagine, or sometimes become vulnerable to, the problem. Many of my students have come and quietly asked to be evaluated. They remind me of the young medical intern who is beset by the maladies he encounters each day. Thus, the study of psychological aberrations is often not a pleasant subject. Many of us are reluctant to seek professional help for fear of finding out that something is wrong. Because of my reluctance to always look for the "fly on the beautiful stained-glass window" I promise to limit this excursion into the dark side. However, my responsibility in the preparation of this book will not be fulfilled unless our understanding of senior adults encompasses flaws as well as strengths.

## Hope!

You may be threatened by the purported complexity of psychological disorders and feel hopeless, especially if you are afflicted or stand beside a loved one who suffers. I am finding more hope day by day. Yes, there is hope! So much can be prevented—so many can be healed! Many can be sustained and gain their great purpose in life by standing even in the midst of perplexing, mysterious problems. David, the great king of Israel, was depressed. An endless number of great spiritual giants have suffered in the throes of melancholy, despair, suicidal ideation, and even schizophrenia. The father of the modern clinical pastoral education movement had three psychotic breaks before he moved into his life's greatest work. Illness may be like a fever—cleansing and burning out the dross. I have seen too many victories to allow you to begin this walk with me without hope. God has blessed with medical skills, the ability to use the more traditional spiritual resources, and other resources (not thought of as spiritual, but given by God), to help in countless ways. We need to know the enemies of our well-being.

## Etiology (Study of Causes)

Now, we need to get back to the inevitable first question, "What caused that problem?" It requires courage to write "there is much uncertainty and disagreement about the causes of psychopathology." However, the theories and experimental studies are not without merit because they have alerted us to a wide range of causes. These causes have been generally categorized under physiological, biochemical, psychological (behavioral), and genetic. The main problem, according to Eric Pfeiffer is the inability of the senior adult to adapt to crises, problems, or losses in these three areas.[1] Thus, one can see a common denominator in the problem of cause. Although problems may arise from different areas of life—the crucial issue is how the senior adult adjusts or adapts to the problem. This idea demonstrates the interrelatedness of man as a living soul. The physical is vitally related to the psychological and sociological. Major works in gerontology usually may be outlined as biological, sociological, and psychological. However, these books have been notorious in that the relationship with God is usually omitted. On their behalf, I must admit that the sociology of human behavior could conceivably subsume spiritual relationships. A brief breakout of some of the discrete areas of cause may be helpful. First, we should examine the physiological cause theory of psychopathology.

*Physiological cause*

The endocrine glands have been noted for their influence in personality development and implications in psychological disorders. The thyroid gland has been related to depression and excited behavior and considered important in sexual functions. The gonads, pituitary, adrenal, and pancreas glands are also extremely important to one's psychological functioning.

The impairment of brain tissue function as seen in the organic brain syndrome produces a wide spectrum of psychological symptoms. The extent of the impairment as well as the state of the individual would determine the severity of the problems. A stroke is an organic brain impairment. As you know, the impairment would vary according to severity. OBS (organic brain syndrome) will be discussed at length later as a separate disorder.

While serving as the coordinator for a mental health center, I received a call one day about a senior adult who had gone berserk. His relatives thought that since the behavior was so greatly disturbed, he should be treated psychologically. I referred him immediately to a physician who found congestive heart failure that had resulted in an inadequate blood supply to the brain. The heart with its essential function is foundational in psychological functioning.

In short, any physiological impairment may be reflected in the nerve centers and appear in psychological symptoms. Some are more directly related to these centers and are thus more potent.

*Biochemical cause*

In known and unknown ways the above mentioned organs and glands have much to do with one's biochemistry. However, a theory about neurotransmitters has captured the thinking of many experts in the biophysical sciences. For this reason the biochemical cause theory will be briefly presented by one who is certainly not an expert. At least a quintet of neurotransmitters has been isolated or postulated. These chemicals relay the electrical charges that follow the nerve cell pathways. An opening between nerve cells called a "synapse" has been theorized. When the neurotransmitters are out of balance, blocked, or too abundant, in the snapse, the result may be dramatic. Either an overwhelming psychotic reaction with excitement and thoughts flying uncontrollably through the mind may occur or the thoughts and movements are retarded to the state of depression. Drugs (psychotropics) are used to block the receptor sites in the synapses or speed up or recycle the neurotransmitters, whichever is needed. One theory of electroconvulsive therapy is that it jolts the electrical system and/or neurotransmitters into proper functioning. The biochemical theory is gaining ascendancy in the mental health field. Some theorists in this tradition maintain that delinquent behavior has a biochemical cause.

*Psychodymanic cause*

The theory that mental disorders are caused by destructive interpersonal relationships and social forces has long been with us. Some leaders within the dynamic and/or spiritual tradition are threatened by the gains made in the other theories of cause which are, in the main, physiological. This threat lacks a base in reality. For years we have observed the chemical alterations that occur as a result of stress. People have been known to accomplish surprising feats when frightened or extremely angry. Thus, psychodynamics may be more fundamental than chemical imbalance.

The reader can see my very obvious bias in favor of the power of the mind and spirit of man, and especially when man is allied with the Supreme Power of the universe.

The psychological needs described in chapter 4 have to do with inter-personal situations. When needs of social involvement, love, and useful-ness are not met, people have problems. The problem may be experi-enced as a deficit at first and then all types of behavior ensue in an attempt to get these deep legitimate needs satisfied. Some types of behavior complicate the problem and further prevent the development of relationships of love and usefulness. Fears, anxieties, depression, hopelessness, hostility, and misguided behavior are some of the psycho-dynamic forces that determine the content of mental disorders. In a nutshell, this is basically the psychodynamic view.

Behavior has been assigned in some writings as the cause of mental disorders. I have chosen to place behavior under the psychodynamic view. If all behavior is communication, whether to self or others, then it is interpersonal and has the possibility of engendering powerful forces in self and others. The issue is whether behavior is more fundamental than psychological needs. Most motivation theories have needs listed as preceding behavior.

## Genetic cause

Usually, mental disorders of the same type are found in successive generations. Because of this finding, researchers have sought to estab-lish a gentic cause. Studies of twins and other successive and immediate family relationships have produced statistics that indicate the strong possibility of a genetic cause. However, just one exception in the study of identical twins is enough to cast doubt on the genetic cause theory. Also, successive generations have similar family organizational pat-terns, values, and other dynamics that may be the predisposing cause.

The reality of genetic physical differences is obvious. Since physiology is vitally interrelated to an individual's psychological functioning, then the constitutional base must, at least, be given serious consideration. The size and functioning ability of the endocrine glands; the quality of the cardiovascular system; and, in fact, the wholistic view of man must consider individual physical differences which can account for psychological differences and vice versa.

To accept partially the findings of the genetic cause theorists and the reality of physical differences and psychological consequences may be depressing. However, I believe that this does not have to be the case in most instances. A self-understanding, physical as well as psychological, flowing out of loving relationships with God and our fellow man, may use deficits as a life-style that can be immensely effective. Of course, self-understanding and nurture are implied to be linked to responsible behavior. Because of physiological differences and some which predispose one to psychological disorders, the individual must be on guard and related to the strength-giving resources found in relationships that are medical as well as spiritual-social.

## Somatogenic Psychological Disorders

"Somatogenic" is an old term which was intended to designate those psychological disorders that result from physiological problems (problems of the body). Much debate swirls around the separation of psychological problems into two groups. Those which have their "genesis from the body" and those which have their "genesis from the psyche or mind." For the sake of simplicity and for deeper reasons, I will hold to these two divisions which say more about cause than the actual problem. Enough has been said about etiology (cause). The following specific psychological problems are presented descriptively. They are found in all age groups including senior adults. The organic brain syndrome is found much more in older persons than in any other age group. Mental retardation is thought to be found much less among senior adults.

The two disorders discussed usually are found to be caused by impairment of brain tissue function or chromosomal abnormality. They may result from severe deprivation or a severe psychogenic or functional psychiatric disorder.

*Organic brain syndrome*

"Organic brain syndrome" is a group if symptoms which develop because of damage to brain tissue. The brain does not function normally and at least five different symptoms can be observed. These symptoms, or mental problems, may be thought of as a cluster of problems which are all present in some degree simultaneously. A variety of tests and close clinical observations may be required for the symptoms to be detected when the damage is slight. When damage to brain tissue has been extensive then the symptoms are obvious. These symptoms, called a "syndrome" are as follows.

*Loss of judgment.*—The individual may not be able to make the proper decision in regard to finances, business dealings, and so forth. The wife of an older man came to me for counseling about family problems. The husband had suffered a recent stroke and was unable to make good judgment decisions in his construction business. Also, the jokes he told at social gatherings were not appropriate. He had never exhibited that type of behavior before.

Not only is there a loss of judgment in decision-making and relationships but in psychomotor functions. Often, the ability to make judgments in spatial matters is affected. One can readily see this in the driving of a person who is intoxicated or in the random ineffectual flailing of a boxer who has been given a severe blow to the head.

*Memory loss.*—Recent memory is affected by damage to brain tissue function. The older memory traces seem to be deeper and more intact while the recent happenings are not associated with earlier memories. This may be due largely to a lack of alertness and directly attributed to a damaged organ, the brain.

*Disorientation.*—Psychological orientation is usually related to a person's ability to function in four spheres of awareness: (1) knowledge of persons around the individual, (2) knowledge of where one is, (3) knowledge of time (hour, day, year), and (4) knowledge of current situations. Several years ago I responded to a call for help in a rural community. The individual thought to be in the most trouble was saying with persuasive and monotonous repetition, "I want to go home and be with Jesus." Over and over again the words were repeated. Standing nearby, as if in shock, was the older husband. I sat down by him, and in an effort to comfort, a conversation was begun. I was amazed to find that he was living in a year that was several years earlier than the current year. He did a good job with the farm chores but he must have been functioning out of habit.

*Liability of mood.*—A distinctive symptom of brain damage is a rapid mood swing. All of us have mood swings and the shifts may occur fairly rapidly. However, the emotions characteristic of the organic brain syndrome are extremely labile. The change may be dramatic and instantaneous.

*Intellectual losses.*—The inability to do mathematical calculations is observed as a result of damage to brain tissue. Since such calculations require a fairly intact recent memory, a correlation is seen between the intellectual and memory losses.

Any impairment of brain tissue affects a person in some area of physical and psychological functioning. However, in many instances organic brain syndrome can be reversed. Robert N. Butler, M.D., said, "The failure to diagnose and treat *reversible brain syndromes* is so unnecessary and yet so widespread that I would caution families of older persons to question doctors involved in care about this."[2] He went on to say that reversible brain syndromes are characterized by various changing levels of awareness rather than a fixed disorientation. "Hallucinations may be present, usually of the visual rather than auditory type. The patient is typically disoriented, mistaking one person for another, and other intellectual functions can also be impaired. Restlessness, unusual aggressiveness or a dazed expression may be noticed."[3]

The organic brain syndrome may be caused by malnutrition, a blow to the head, tumors, intracranial infection, metabolism, persistent high blood pressure, intoxicants, dehydration, congestive heart failure, cerebrovascular accidents, arteriosclerosis, atherosclerosis, reactions to surgery, and many other agents which disturb brain tissue function. One study reported by Sister Michael Sibille indicated that 75 percent of a sample of senior adults who suffered from chronic, irreversible brain syndromes could have been reversed by early detection and treatment.[4] The main reason for writing this scary review of the organic brain syndrome is to offer some reassurance as to the possibilities of a measure of success in treatment.

Professor Frank Minkoff, a 70-year-old Russian immigrant with a university degree in engineering, was still teaching mathematics at an evening school. He was unmarried, the only member of his family in the United States and lived in an apartment crammed with books. Suddenly he became confused and disoriented. He was frightened and refused to leave his room. Concerned neighbors quickly called a doctor, who expressed his unwillingness to make a home visit saying, "There is nothing I can do. He needs to be in a nursing home or a mental institution." The neighbors were unconvinced, remembering Mr. M.'s earlier good functioning. They pleaded with the doctor and, under pressure, he angrily complied and visited the home. While there he again repeated his conviction that Mr. M. needed "custodial" care. Mr. M. was coherent enough to refuse, saying he would never voluntarily go to a nursing home or mental hospital. He did agree to be admitted to a medical hospital. Admission took place and studies resulted in the diagnosis "reversible brain syndrome due to acute viral infection." Mr. M. was successfully treated and released to his home in good condition in less than a week.[5]

True senility is when an organic syndrome has become irreversible. This, of course, is not a myth. Butler refers to two major conditions that create the mental disorders often termed "senility." "One is cerebral arteriosclerosis (hardening of the arteries of the brain); the other, unfortunately referred to as senile brain disease, is due to a mysterious dissolution of brain cells."[6]

There are three by-products of the organic brain syndrome. First, one's ability to function in specific ways is impaired. Second, psychological reactions to these deficits are present in the form of depression, doubt, loss of confidence, and so forth. Third, underlying personality problems are released because of a lack of control. Prior to the brain impairment the individual could control unacceptable impulses and the resultant behavior.

An individual with a healthy personality developed in a Christian home, church, and properly related to Christ has an advantage. Were he to suffer from a brain syndrome he would likely have less of the ugly, unmanageable release phenomena that one sees sometimes when the underlying personality is disordered.

## Mental retardation of senior adults

In the major works of gerontology, mental retardation of senior adults is scarcely mentioned. In addition, during the past few decades leaders in the field of mental retardation have focused on the needs of children and young adults and have rarely given attention to the older population. The Institute of Gerontology at the University of Michigan has recently become aware that the population of senior adults who are retarded is increasing. Through medical care this segment of our population will show substantial increases in the 1980's. A survey of mentally retarded patients in Michigan institutions revealed that approximately one percent of that particular population was senior adults. Recent community placement of many hospital patients weakens the reliability of the survey in determining the actual number of retarded senior adults within the total population.

As in the organic brain syndrome, numerous levels of functioning may be seen in mental retardation. Usually, the causes for OBS and MR are similar. A striking difference is that in mental retardation the damage to brain tissue function occurred during the early developmental period. Because of this impairment, learning, speech, and social development were slowed down.

The retarded senior adult has distinctive needs when compared to others in nursing homes and institutions. He may not have a progressive impairment and thus be fairly stable. Also, with sensory losses he may be in double or triple jeopardy.

I was pleased in my research to find that Mr. Horace Kerr, supervisor of the Senior Adult Division at the Sunday School Board of the Southern Baptist Convention, presented the opening remarks at a 1976 conference titled, "Gerontological Aspects of Mental Retardation." Since 1974 gerontological associations have begun some work in this neglected area.

## Psychogenic, Psychological, and Physical Disorders

The above subheading is deliberately used to make explicit the interrelatedness of mind and body or the interrelatedness of the spiritual and psychophysiological. Later, a brief presentation of a nomenclature (naming of disorders) will be presented that has to do with a spiritual etiology or cause. This emphasis was mentioned as related to psychodynamic cause.

In this section, depression (suicide), manic behavior, paranoid reactions, mind-body problems, situational disturbances, drug abuse and alcoholism, and other disorders are discussed.

## Depression

Senior adults are often affected by depression, the same disorder that afflicts approximately one-third of our total population. Dr. William Pinson, Jr., addressing the Southern Baptist Annuity Board said,

Feeling unloved, unwanted and guilty about being nonproductive, many older persons slip into depression. As friends die and family members move away, loneliness may settle like a thick dark cloud. More than one-third live alone or with nonrelatives. Most older women are widows. Other problems compound the sense of frustration. Over three million are illiterate. Only 50 percent have a high school education; only 5 percent attended college. Many just give up. Suicide and mental illness rates high among the elderly, especially the men.[7]

Depression has been described psychiatrically as an affective disorder. "Affective" or "affect" has to do with feeling tone. Thus, depression is usually described as a "down feeling." Dr. Charles Feraci, a psychiatrist friend and supervisor at Southeast Louisiana Hospital, taught me to look for "D's" in determining whether an individual is depressed or not. He died while yet a young man but I will remember him in this way.

Several of the "D's" are as follows:

(1) Disillusionment—possibly the senior adult has seen someone, themselves, or the worth of an event or activity for actually what it is and this may not have been a positive revelation. The high standards of recent cohorts of senior adults have made more probable the incidence of disillusionment.

(2) Disappointment—the resultant attitude or feelings that occur when expectations are not met. I will never forget an insight given to me by a Catholic priest at a workshop that I was leading in West Alabama.

It was my understanding that he was recuperating from a heart attack, and this fact made his particular comments especially insightful to me. When discussing depression and its implications for our Christian faith he said, "I believe that depression may be the result of the sin of presumptiveness." He elaborated on this simple but profound statement. "Our expectations may be unrealistic, unreasonable, and we may be presuming on God to accomplish what might be self-centered goals." The book of Habakkuk and, in fact, the Bible from cover to cover illustrates a depression that occurs as a result of our expectations about what God ought to do for us. G. Campbell Morgan stated that Habakkuk 2:4 is the greatest sentence in the Book of God:[8] "The just shall live by his faith." The prophet applied this great truth to his own depression. It is not a faith that God will do exactly thus and so, but a faith that God's providence will prevail. Can you see how tempted I am as I write to get into a Christian therapy for the psychological problems of senior adults? But I had hoped that this would not be a "how-to" book but a "who-are-they" book (Understanding Senior Adults). Now, back to the listing of "D's." The prefix "dis" gives us a clue to many other words that describe depression. These words with the prefix are the opposite of confidence and self-esteem.

(3) Despair—frustration and fatigue about life is diffused throughout the personality. If depression were placed on some type of continuum, despair may be at the extreme toward "very serious." Also, despair may be differentiated from depression in that it may be an overtaxing of the physical powers to a point of desperation. Desperation is another "D" that will help us conceptualize depression and expand our concept of despair.

(4) Discouraged—the loss of courage in regard to one's life situation usually involves a discouraging relationship with persons. Courage is the ability to continue even though you are afraid.

(5) Doubt—the uncertainity about one's competence, will-being, and acceptance by others is prevalent. "Depressed patients often experience difficulty in making decisions, even minor ones, and their thought processes and speech are significantly slowed down as are their physical movements."[9]

(6) Diminished self-esteem—one's sense of self-worth has deteri-
orated. A wide discrepancy exists between one's self-image (the way
one sees himself) and the ideal self that he thinks that he should be. The
greater the distance between how one sees himself now and what he
ought to be, the lower the self-esteem. Consider the implications of this
statement at retirement and in the other adjustment tasks of senior
adults.

(7) Desolation—"Depressed patients experience vivid dreams of being
lost and lonely in isolated, frightening, desolate places."[10]

Other interesting words that begin with the letter "D" may help us
further conceptualize depression. Disconsolate, despondency, dis-
traught, and destitute may be thought of as synonyms or closely related
words which are assigned particular "down" meanings by different
people. Words do not have meanings, they are given meanings in the
mind of the individual. Thus, it is hoped that this play on words may help
in understanding depression, a disorder that is episodic in nature and
afflicts so many senior adults. Accompanying the psychological attitudes
and feelings revealed in the list of "D's" are the basic physical signs of
depression, such as loss of weight, sleep, appetite, energy, and the
problem of constipation.

Many authorities consider depression and anger closely related. One
theory of suicide is that the depressed person turns the anger on himself. This statement may seem to contradict statements made later in
the brief description of suicide. In effect, the statement indicates that
suicides of the young are usually hostile acts against a loved object.
Whereas the suicides of senior adults are not contrived to punish
anyone. Knowing that depression is the chief cause of senior adult suicide, and subscribing to the anger-depression relationship, we may be
hardpressed to prove that senior adults are not motivated by hostility.
However, most senior adults who commit or attempt suicide have been
diagnosed as psychotic and irrational and thus would possibly lack the
premeditated hostility of the young.

*Suicide.*—Seventy-five percent of persons who commit suicide or
attempt suicide are depressed. The U.S. Public Health Service reported
in 1975 that suicide rates for senior adults were between 42 to 62 percent

higher than those of the general population. One reason for the higher rate is that senior adults are more effective at actually committing suicide.[11] Pfeiffer reports that when senior adults attempt suicide "he/she almost always fully intends to die."[12] Suicide attempts of younger persons often are hostile acts. This is not the case with senior adults. Rescue of senior adults is often accidental. This would possibly indicate a genuine desire to die rather than to punish a loved one. Senior adults who make suicide attempts and fail should be placed immediately in the hospital.[13] It is true that any indication of suicide potential must be taken seriously for all age groups. It is especially true for senior adults. All studies have shown that a male Caucasian, living alone, suffering from a chronic illness and the recent loss of a significant person has the greatest suicide potential. "As is true in younger years, in old age, too, the suicidal intent is usually temporary. If a person can be helped through a stressful period toward a new and satisfying adjustment, a life will have been saved."[14]

If people were asked to guess if suicide is common in old age, they would probably answer no, and the reason they might give would be that senior adults are not usually given to very violent actions—that they are fairly conservative. This is one of the arguments that I have used through the years in viewing the older people who have associated themselves together in view of political change. Because of slight sensory deprivations and possibly less intense emotions, senior adults are not as difficult to deal with in their associations, but this is not true in regard to suicide. Suicide is more common in the higher age groups in many countries of the Western civilization. There is, however, one exception, there is little suicide in extreme old age. The difference between the male and female varies much with the culture in which they live. However, just as in all of our Western cultures, the general tendency is for older males to be more suicidal. If you were to analyze some of the causes, the major cause seems to be not so much because of chronic physical conditions or terminal illness, and so forth, but it has been related to a depressive disorder.[15]

Another interesting phenomenon is that suicidal senior adults do not come from the delinquent and more transient segments of our population, instead they have a history of satisfactory work records. A broken home in childhood seems to play a significant part in many suicide attempts. This is more true for young people than for senior adults. The greatest number of older people who commit suicide are suffering from a psychosis, in other words, they could probably be diagnosed as of unsound mind and they would be within two categories, the depressive states or impairment of brain tissue function. There is no doubt that the majority of them are suffering from depression and these things may be seen together—depression, insomnia, tension, and agitation. The majority of them are suffering from depression rather than from the organic brain syndrome.[16]

Most senior adults are suffering from chronic physical illnesses or disability at the time of self-injury, the physical problems are not really the precipitating factors in the suicide or suicide attempts. Certainly, the physiological problems such as are seen in the organic brain syndrome diminish control over conduct, inhibitions are weakened, and fatigue occurs which also diminishes the general resistance of the individual to stress. These physiological problems certainly bring about feelings of depression and certainly are related to the suicide or suicide attempts. Most senior adults dread helplessness more than death. Seemingly there is a sudden realization that they have become old or that they are through with life and this seems to be an intolerable burden for them. In spite of these very significant physiological factors, research seems to indicate that the most crucial determining factor for suicide is the result of mental disorders. Of course, these disorders cannot be separated from the circumstances and situations which have emotional consequences.[17]

A person who is suicidal whether he is old or young should never be quickly discharged from a hospital in the belief that what he has done was really a mistake or that having learned a lesson he will not try it again.[18] This is very dangerous and I have learned in personal psychotherapy that the individual who has attempted suicide is in danger for at least ninety days after that attempt. He may for a period of time appear to be very guilty about what he has done and there may be a flight to health and a kind of calmness and peace come over him, but at that time he may be in greatest danger of suicide.

*Manic behavior*

One category for psychological disturbances is "manic-depressive." The depressive reactions discussed in this chapter may also be seen related in this disorder. Depression may be the low side of manic states—excited activity. The literature pictures the manic as being extremely circumstantial (mentioning all details of an event) and feels like he is "on top of the world." Words are flying and usually are used to describe great and grandiose plans. The language has usually been termed as a "flight of ideas." In some older manic patients the generally observed joviality is replaced by a general irritability, punctuated by short outbursts of anger or even of paranoid thinking.[19]

Recently, lithium carbonate has been used successfully to treat this disorder. When taking the drug, close medical supervision is required. The manic disorder has usually been recognized as cyclic in nature. This is true not only in its persistent reoccurrence every two or three years but also in the mood shifts from high to low which may be seen in some expressions of the disorder.

Most of us have highs and lows in our daily lives. However, a manic reaction, as described above, is one in which their person's behavior may be bizarre. The conduct may be unbecoming and antisocial. The person is out of touch with reality. The disorder is termed a "psychosis."

*Paranoid reactions*

"Paranoid" usually connotes extreme sickness. However, in today's world there may be a healthy paranoia. The word, when analyzed, has been given the simple meaning, a "mind that is beside itself"—*para-nois.* The concept, paranoia, filled in through psychiatric and general observations now usually refers to suspiciousness, aloofness, and distrust. It may be a learned behavior that is deeply ingrained and derived from our parents. Various levels of intensity of this type of paranoia are seen but they are usually not of a delusional quality. Severe types of paranoid reactions may be seen in the organic brain syndrome, the involutional (change of life) depressions, specific paranoid states, and in the schizophrenic disorder. I am of the belief that the learned paranoia (copied) by itself may never break out into the delusional paranoia which is often so destructive. However, when learned paranoia is complicated by low self-esteem and physiological deficits, a severe deterioration may occur especially when the individual is under great stress. The Jonestown type may be primarily a disorder of youth. Senior adults do not appear to have such a hostile paranoid orientation.

Senior adults who suffer from vision and hearing losses may be more suspicious than ever before. Any noise may be a prowler and the loss of keys or glasses may be projected onto neighbors or even family members. Insecurities developed from newspaper reports of robbings and killings may heighten suspiciousness. Money may be hidden in books and all about the house. Hiding places may be forgotten as a result of some impairment and thus new suspicions develop. In many instances even the more severe reactions can be reversed through lighting, locks, companionship, and other practical methods. Chemotherapy of a tonic type may be acceptable to the suspicious senior adult. The caution that is so necessary for survival in today's world has been heightened for many senior adults who live alone. Very few of us would fare well if we were alone, weak, and unable to see or hear well and lived in a frail structure. Try it for twenty-five years!

## Mind over body disorders

The formal name for these combination mind and body problems is "psychophysiological and autonomic visceral disorders." The older term used was "psychosomatic." They may be described as physical problems which occur because of persistent or intense emotions that affect one or more of the organ systems. All systems are affected by intense and persistent emotional reactions. It is reasonable that some types of emotional response may affect particular systems and that weak organ systems are particularly vulnerable to distress and even positive intense emotions. The organ systems are: skin, musculoskeletal, respiratory, cardiovascular, hemic and lymphatic, gastro-intestinal, genito-urinary, endocrine, and organ of the special sense.[20] Some of the disorders that may occur are neurodermatosis, backache, bronchial asthma, hypertension, peptic ulcer, and impotence. Many other physical symptoms are listed in the DSM-II. These conditions are diagnosed as psychologically caused only when emotional factors play a causative role.[21]

We have already seen how stress and the intense distress of crises have physiological implications. The particular disorders mentioned in this section are related to the independent nervous system—the system which innervates the various organ systems without our conscious control. In all probability, a large percentage of the general health problems of senior adults are the mind-body type. The problems may have been reoccuring over the years and thus a chronic health problem develops as one organ system is seriously impaired.

If I were to choose the most significant psychological disorder about which to alert senior adults, it would be this particular type of problem. It is extremely common, affecting all of us, and usually not as complex and deep as other psychological problems but may be very painful and eventually, even fatal.

## Situational disturbances

The transient situational disturbances of psychiatric literature are, in reality, the adjustment of individuals to disturbing situations. The intense adjustment tasks of senior adults were discussed in chapter 5. It is possible that the word *transient* used in psychiatric nomenclature is misleading. The point has been made that even when a crisis of adjustment may have passed, there is every possibility that the adjustment could have been a maladjustment. Technically, the crisis situation may be transient(not lasting) but the maladjustment or good adjustment may have permanence.

## Drug abuse and alcoholism

One of the causes of confusion and disorganization is drugs. All of us have seen the intoxicating (poisoning) effects of alcohol. Other mind-altering chemicals do the same thing. Dr. Wenell Lipscomb, Berkeley psychiatrist, has indicated that the abuse of drugs by senior adults is a growing concern for doctors.

Some senior adults are attempting to escape from loneliness and boredom. Others are unintentional victims of the "spaced-out grandma" syndrome—bizarre behavior which comes about by the combination of certain drugs. These drugs may be those prescribed for the ailments of old age. The multiple prescriptions often produce a cocktail of different drugs which can cause strange behavior. The result may be a chemical psychosis, which clears up when the person is taken off the drugs.[22]

Here again we see the consequences of physical agents which have much to do with psychological symptoms. However, the more fundamental problem in drug abuse and alcoholism may be an underlying psychological cause. Senior adults who fail to relate properly and meet the crises of senior age constructively may resort to the abuse of drugs and alcohol as a means of escape. Alcohol has been one of the world's most used tranquilizers. Underlying depression or anxiety may be temporarily relieved through the use of alcohol. "In such instances the individual is essentially trying to treat his basic psychiatric disturbance, using alcohol as an antidepressant or tranquilizer. Chronic alcohol abuse can result in chronic organic brain syndromes of the Korsakoff's type."[23] Some authorities believe that one of the main contributors to brain deficits in senior adults may be their use of alcohol. Also, intoxication and withdrawal have a much greater lethal potential in senior adults.[24]

*Other disorders*

A complete description of all psychological problems in detail is not feasible. Several are particularly relevant to a better understanding of senior adults. These are schizophrenia, hypochondriasis, anxiety, and insomnia.

*Schizophrenia.* — It may be a futile attempt to even mention such an all-encompassing disorder as "schizophrenia." The word, a sometimes overused label, has literally frightened people into some of the symptoms of the disorder. Less than one half of one percent of the total population has been diagnosed as schizophrenic but this percentage amounts to over one million persons — many who are senior adults. They fill the mental hospital geriatric wards, facilities, and the twenty-four thousand nursing homes in the United States. Over one half the population of our mental hospitals are diagnosed as schizophrenic.

The word has been coined to refer to a splitting of the mind. This is not intended to mean that the "splitting" is into separate personalities similar to the *Three Faces of Eve* or the *Sybil* of a recent movie. This type has been considered a neurosis and resembles amnesia. The multiple personalitiess are theoretically a dividing of the personality into distinct personalities. Schizophrenia is not this kind of division. It's division or split is seen between feeling and thinking. There is either a blunted mood or flat mood when it is not appropriate or the mood may be exactly the opposite from the one that is appropriate to the intellectual situation. When frightened the person may laugh or sometimes be smiling for no reason at all. The technical definition is "the intellectual content is inconsonant with the affect."

Traditionally, four fundamental symptoms have been given and listed as four "A's."

(1) Associations are loose. The person rambles from one thought to another with no real continuity of associations.

(2) Affect is inappropriate. The mood does not fit the situation. The person may be talking about a serious situation and all the while be laughing.

(3) Autistic. The individual is in a world of fantasy that is of his own construction. He literally lives in a dream world.

(4) Ambivalence is severe. Ambivalence is the holding of two contrary emotions simultaneously. In severe ambivalence, love and hate may stalemate each other. Such a condition is difficult to conceptualize but the indecision and conflict seen in adolescence gives us some idea of the potency of this symptom.

*Hypochondriasis.*—The word was originally intended to mean "a condition that existed below the ribs." Now, the multiple body complaints that characterize hypochondriasis has spread to include the total body. It may be a learned behavior that came from mother and father, a displacement of anxiety about the world into a physiological symptom, or a bizarre delusional preoccupation with a "hole in one's throat."

Eric Pfeiffer, psychiatrist and noted gerontologist, believes that hypochondriasis, as a problem for senior adults, is frequent enough to be placed third in line behind paranoid reactions and depression. He considers the major dynamic of the disorder to stem from an inability of the individual to find satisfaction in the world of relationships around him.

Thus, the person as a result of unmet psychological needs becomes intensely preoccupied with his own body. Also, there is the possibility that he may gain the attention of others. But he is extremely resistent to the idea that his problem is psychological.[25]

*Anxiety.* — Anxiety has been characterized as a vague unfocused fear or dread. However, it is usually differentiated from fear. Anxiety is unfocused whereas fear is focused on a known object.

The plight of some senior adults with their isolation and sensory deprivation add to a world that may be largely unfocused. Anxiety may be an almost constant companion of senior adults as they face the severe adjustment tasks and decisions about alternatives. The anxiety that underlies paranoia may also be fundamental to depression. It is the chief emotional response that underlies other neuroses and may be displaced into phobias, compulsive behavior, hypochondriasis, neurasthenia, traumatic attacks of dread and breathlessness, and even seeing and hearing loss. Anxiety, so pervasive in our culture, is one of the strongest influences in our mind-body problems discussed in this chapter.

*Insomnia.* — Many senior adults are more concerned about sleeplessness rather than too much sleep. Pfeiffer has this to say about the changing sleep patterns of senior adults.

> Clinicians should be aware that this changed sleep pattern of more frequent awakenings, less deep sleep, and several naps during the daytime is the normal sleep pattern for aging persons and that this normal pattern should not be disturbed through the regular use of sleeping medication to keep the person asleep eight hours throughout the night or by preventing the elderly person from taking short naps during the daytime hours.[26]

The patterns become more pronounced and of striking inconsistency when a psychiatric disorder is present. The use of drugs can help, but studies in the biology of aging emphasize the importance of minimum dosages and temporary use. Drugs are not eliminated by senior adults as well as by younger persons.

## Disorders and Views of God

A psychiatrist of great renown has become concerned about what has become of sin. Many giants in the field of psychology from Jung forward have suggested that beneath many of the problems of living, especially the dynamic, functional, psychological problems, are religious concerns. I am not saying that all sickness is sin, but it is not the wholeness or holiness that God desires. Jesus has taught us that all calamity and sickness is not the result of sin. However, I am seeing more every day what a healthy, Christian view of God can mean to a living soul and especially to his psychological functioning.

Recently, I have become extremely impressed with the writings of Paul Pruyser, a clinical psychologist from the Menninger Clinic. He has suggested a diagnostic nomenclature that is vitally related to psychiatric terms but is distinctively theological. He has suggested the following guidelines for pastoral diagnosis:

(1) An assessment is made of the person's awareness of the Holy. What does the individual consider to be sacred?

(2) An exploration is made of the individual's understanding of the providence of God as it is directly related to him.

(3) Elicit a description of the individual's faith. How does his faith allow him to function?

(4) What is the individual's understanding of grace as it relates to him?

(5) How does the individual experience repentance?

(6) Assess whether the person experiences communion or is estranged.

(7) An assessment is made of the person's sense of mission or vocation in life.

I am impressed with these diagnostic guidelines which help us to see many psychological problems in relationship to God. I have long considered the anxiety and resultant neuroses as nothing but attempts of an individual to control the world by himself. The unresolved guilt and the conflict of values are all so much a part of depression and anxiety. A Christian psychology must be refined which can help senior adults determine the improper relationship and the proper relationship to God. It must also refine and utilize the resources of truth, whether in psychiatry or in our Christian heritage, to help senior adults develop the proper relationship to God.

NOTES

[1]Eric Pfeiffer, "Psychopathology and Social Pathology," in *Handbook of the Psychology of Aging*, p. 650.

[2]Butler, *Why Survive?* pp. 175-76.

[3]Ibid., p. 176.

[4]Sibille, *Psychosocial Aspects of Aging*, Film, Part 2.

[5]Butler, *Why Survive?* p. 5.

[6]Ibid., p. 10.

[7]William W. Pinson, "Aging a Christian Response," *Search* (Fall 1975), p. 7.

[8]G. Campbell Morgan, *The Triumphs of Faith: Expositions of Hebrews 11* (Grand Rapids: Baker Book House, 1973, reprint ed.), p. 13.

[9]Eric Pfeiffer, "Psychopathology," p. 653.

[10]Ibid.

[11]Cary S. Kart, Eileen S. Metress, and James F. Metress, *Aging and Health: Biologic and Social Perspectives* (Menlo Park, Ca.: Addison-Wesley Publishing, Inc., 1978), p. 186.

[12]Eric Pfeiffer, "Psychopathology," p. 655.

[13]Ibid.

[14]Ewald W. Busse and Eric Pfeiffer, *Functional Psychiatric Disorders in Old Age, Behavior and Adapation in Late Life*, 2nd ed. (Boston: Little, Brown and Company, 1977), p. 179.

[15]Edwin S. Shneidman and Norman L. Farberow, eds. *Clues to Suicide* (New York: McGraw-Hill Book Co., Inc., 1957), p. 143.

[16]Ibid., p. 145.

[17]Ibid., p. 146.

[18]Ibid., p. 150.

[19]Pfeiffer, "Psychopathology," p 655.

[20]The Committee on Nomenclature and Statistics of the American Psychiatric Association, *DSM-II, Diagnostic and Statistical Manual of Mental Disorders* (Washington, D.C.: American Psychiatric Assoicaition, 1968), pp. 46-47.

[21]Ibid.

[22]*The Times-Picayune*, New Orleans, Louisiana, October 24, 1976.

[23]Pfeiffer, "Psychopathology," p. 659.

[24]Ibid.

[25]Ibid., p. 657.

[26]Ibid., p. 659.

# 7

# Psychological Implications

When I write of psychological implications, a great hope wells up within me. It is that senior adults, members of their families, and others for whom this book has been written will realize in some ways how they are psychologically implicated in the well-being of senior adults.

A Christian psychology of aging moves beyond the mental and spiritual functioning of senior adults to encompass the thoughts, actions, and feelings of others about aging. This speaks of a broad psychology of aging. Without such a breadth of view the individual senior adult cannot be understood within the context of his crucial interpersonal existence. Nor could he be changed or the psychology of community be changed—a psychology which has been so influential.

Numerous references have indicated how much community attitudes about senior adults affect the process of growing old. I have discussed also the impact of positive and negative attitudes and relationships. Persistent efforts to help them remain useful are invaluable. This has not always been the case, because many senior adults have been shelved either by themselves or others. As a consequence, we have not been able to benefit from the wealth of talent that has been lost. Because of this I am reminded of a stanza from Thomas Gray's "Ellegy Written in a Country Churchyard."

> Full many a gem of purest ray serene,
> The dark unfathomed caves of ocean bear;
> Full many a flower is born to blush unseen,
> And waste its sweetness on the desert air.

The isolation of many senior adults is like unto a dark ocean cave. Their beauties are often seen only by their pets.

*You caused it!*

Blaming others is a major preoccupation of many, and even a few senior adults. A tendency has existed in gerontology to point an accusing finger at society about the condition of senior adults. "If you had not fallen in love with the beauty of youth and the glories of power, senior adults would not have been disenfranchised." "We (senior adults) have to struggle to survive in spite of 'ageism,' 'myths,' and all types of road-blocks that you have put in our way."

You can be certain that the powerful psychological defense mechanism (projection = blaming others) of childhood is still at work in the general psychology of aging. One strong implication is that aging and all other age groups may be separated into two groups. The groups will be facing each other in a dual of retaliation. The sad result is that no one really wins.

*We caused it!*

When couples and families come for counseling and say, "We caused it," my hopes for change are heightened. "We caused it," is not enough, but it is a good beginning point for correcting group problems. The same applies for the difficulties senior adults experience directly. In fact, when a hand is injured, the entire person suffers. When one member of a family has problems they usually are understood to be an outgrowth of a family problem. Also, problems in the lives of senior adults reflect the problems of our society. So, in effect, *we* are all party to it. The recent emphases on the interrelatedness of universe systems, family systems, and all types of systems has helped us to understand a process that is more than a one to one cause and effect problem. The problems that senior adults face are a pustule on the body of a sick society. Yet, this is not to say that no one is responsible! We are all responsible under God to help order our system according to a Christian design.

No doubt, other age groups have communicated to senior adults their displeasure about the use of excessive authority. A type of harsh domination by our elders continues to exist in various areas of our society. A tyranny of years may have prevailed and thus covert and overt conflicts have ensued. The changing of role relationships necessitates a change in the rules of relationships. The roles for senior adults are not understood. This means that the rules for relationships are not understood. Such is true for those relating to the senior adult as it is for the senior adult himself. Therefore, we do not know the rules, or, who should make the rules, or, who should be in charge of the rules. Is it any wonder that the growing number of senior adults would develop more conflicts within our society?

The psychological implication moves from blaming others to guilt when we, senior adults and others, realize our part in the unhealthy drama of struggling oldsters and youngsters.

Senior adult problems are the flip side of the problems of those to whom they relate. The depressions of senior adults inspire the hostility of their children and the hostilities of their children inspire the senior adult depressions. Which came first? Attempts to assign blame upon the one that first began this vicious cycle are futile. Now, it has become a process that is almost instantaneous and perennial.

The acceptance of guilt (real guilt) can be the beginning of healing. Guilt has two expressions, fact and feeling. In real guilt both will be present. However, condemnation and the fostering of heavy guilt feelings seem to work against correcting our mistakes. Thus, the fact of guilt is sufficient if we sincerely want to correct the senior adult situation in our society. We shall find that a more fundamental problem of relationship to God and others lies beneath the "ageism." Yet, dealing deeply with the ageism of young and old may force us to a Supreme Value.

## We can all win!

I am deeply appreciative of the "no lose method" presented in the writings of Thomas Gordon, author of books for those who are related significantly to children.[1] A solution to the complex problems of senior adults will be a solution to many of the problems of other age groups. Whether working with couples, families, senior adults, or competing groups I believe that the possibility of everyone winning is real! No one should lose! Of course, such an idealistic view hinges upon the values held by the differing individuals or groups.

Our need for each other can be seen clearly in the giving of gifts. The needs of persons and the gifts of persons may complement each other. An old Balinese legend may help illustrate the "all can win method" that is possible in Christ.

It is said that once upon a time the people of a remote mountain village used to sacrifice and eat their old men. A day came when there was not a single old man left, and the traditions were lost. They wanted to build a great house for the meetings of the assembly, but when they came to look at the tree-trunks that had been cut for that purpose no one could tell the top from the bottom: if the timber were placed the wrong way up, it would set off a series of disasters. A young man said that if they promised never to eat the old men anymore, he would be able to find a solution. They promised. He brought his grandfather, whom he had hidden; and the old man taught the community to tell top from bottom.[2]

### Changed Attitudes

One of the hoped for changes that should come out of a study of aging would be changed attitudes. Superficial and occasional acts of kindness do not necessarily indicate changed attitudes. Among the psychological implications are changed perceptions of senior adults. From accurate perceptions the senior adult will be conceptualized more realistically. Our behavior/communications will reflect these realistic appraisals and more appropriate attitudes will be formed. This is something of the steps required for attitudinal changes.

Basically, the attitude about the entire life cycle as having growth potential rather than only decline is hoped for. Tournier maintained that "life is a task to be accomplished. But who can claim that he has accomplished his task, that he has finished his task? The task always remains unfinished.[3] Here, Tournier is speaking mainly of the attitude of acceptance that is so sorely needed in senior adults who have regrets about unfulfilled tasks. However, the reasoning behind the acceptance of unfulfilled tasks is that much can be done and needs to be done until the end.

Possibly a changed attitude about death may change our attitudes about age. They are so closely associated. The fearlessness about death that is claimed for most senior adults *may* be true but it is not true for the younger age groups. The taboo and threatening bias against age cannot be removed until we deal properly with death. In a Christian psychology hopefully one sees the victory over physical death and spiritual/psychological death that destroys the abundant life. The psychopathologies discussed in chapter 6 are distinguishable from physical death only by degree. Tournier wrote that "people are reluctant to talk about old age and death because they are afraid of emotion, and they willingly avoid the things they feel most emotion about."[4]

The attitude that youth only is beautiful may be changed as one grows to see the profound beauty of old age. Have you seen the beautiful wrinkles of age placed there by years of hard work and sacrifice? I have held tenderly my mother's tiny wrinkled and worn hands. As I held them, I turned back in my mind to the days of the old washpot, the scrub board, the immaculate floors, and our stiff-starched homemade clothes. They rubbed me raw, but I will always appreciate them for the love they symbolized. Those hands pumped the water, cleaned the yard, braved the wood cook stove, and gently caressed my head and body in my sicknesses. The face, the hands, the feet are all symbols of giving—exhausted now, not shapely, but strangely beautiful.

Not discounting the value of activity, hopefully, attitudes have been changed about busy-ness. Such an attitudinal change will mean much to me, to those preparing for age, and those who have arrived. You can hear, "work has never hurt anyone." You must qualify this statement from several perspectives. The individual can destroy himself in his work and thus age prematurely or die. Ethel Sabin Smith, who taught continuously for forty-five years, said:

This ability to be quietly busy is an art which some people never learn. Neither the worker on the assembly line nor the high-powered executive ordinarily learns it. It is opposed to a lifetime of habits acquired by the alert businessman. The driven district attorney often thinks the only alternative to frantic activity is to fall into a merciful sleep. Yet the art of relaxed industriousness is something every old person could cultivate, or else—

The old person must learn to achieve the golden mean between rash activity and supine surrender.[5]

In recent years longitudinal studies have overcome many of the negative attitudes about the competencies of senior adults. The older texts and references to a psychology of aging were dismal. In fact, most of the materials had more to do with senile dementia and had very few positive notes. Fortunately, the newer studies (longitudinal) have shown older Americans to be, in the main, intelligent, sexual, and often, possessing far more information than younger age groups. Thus, an important implication of these studies is that positive attitudes should be reserved for senior-adult competencies until proven differently. In the past because of very obvious deterioration of some older persons the burden of proof has been on those attempting to prove their competencies. Only recently have we become convinced of the almost unaffected learning capacity of senior adults.

A changing of negative attitudes of senior adults about their peers is needed. At times, older persons are the worst enemies of their own age group. Particular attitudinal changes may be needed in regard to sex, financial assistance, and so on. Many of these needed changes may be distinctive of groups of persons in different communities.

## Mending Fences and Finding Forgiveness

I am unwilling to put my head in the sand and deny our society's implication in the problems of senior adults. Nor, for that matter, can senior adults be excused. Simply stated, we are guilty! Weeping and wailing and holding our heads in our hands will only convince a few of our contriteness. The problem will remain unrectified. To convince ourselves of good intentions and absolve ourselves of guilt we need to make restitution. Not only are good works our best guilt removers, they help people, senior adults and ourselves. Thus, a major psychological implication is coping with our guilt while at the same time meeting needs. The psychological rewards of such positive endeavors are immense. Through reparation a deep sense of forgiveness can be experienced. A major implication is that because of our guilt many helpers may make extreme efforts to repair damages. As noted in chapter 1, many do-gooders may be undercutting the independence of senior adults.

I can envision sturdy fences protecting senior adults from exploitation. The insights developed through years of struggle and discipline may be lost unless the fences are in good repair. The gladness of life may be stolen away and the emptiness of depression is all that is left. The fence not only keeps out hostile forces such as hopelessness, suspiciousness, unforgiveness, confusion, and fear, it reminds one of his limitations. Fences define the boundaries of one's territory. It keeps one from minding others' business, from running too fast and too far, and to be aware of a hedge beyond which countless destructive activities may be engaged in.

## New proclamation fence posts

The Scriptures have boundless potential for sermons on aging. The Ten Commandments, the patriarchs, the child of Abraham and Sarah, the call of Moses, the wisdom potential of age, are but a few of the examples found. Sermons can be powerful instruments for changes in attitudes. The principles inherent in the Scripture passages about aging are true in life beyond the confines of the church. The words of educators, family members, senior adults, and other community leaders should parallel the positive notes, challenges, and admonitions found in the pulpit proclamations about senior adults. Some of the fence posts have been knocked down or rotted and need to be replaced. Most of the standing, sturdy posts are applicable to all age groups, but some have particular relevancy for senior adults. One post needs to be rechecked constantly. It is the post that points to the special significance of growing older gracefully. I doubt that the majority of senior adults have achieved this goal, but it is a worthy one! I am reminded of a perceptive older female who prayed,

Lord, thou knowest better than I know myself that I am growing older, and will some day be old. Keep me from getting talkative, and particularly from the fatal habit of thinking I must say something on every occasion. Release me from craving to try to straighten out everybody's affiars. Make me thoughtful, but not moody; helpful but not bossy.

With the vast store of wisdom it seems a pity not to use it all—but thou knowest, Lord, that I want a few friends at the end. Keep my mind free from the recital of endless details—give me the wings to get to the point.

Seal my lips to my many aches and pains—they are increasing and my love of rehearsing them is becoming sweeter as the years go by. I ask for grace enough to listen to the toils of others' pains. Help me to endure them with patience.

Teach me the glorious lesson that occasionally it is possible that I may be mistaken. Keep me reasonably sweet, I do not want to be a saint—some of them are so hard to live with, but a sour old woman is one of the crowning works of the devil.

Help me to extract all possible fun out of life. There are so many funny things around us, and I don't want to miss any of them. Amen.

As I look down the fence, I see another post that leans over so far until the wire resembles a hammock. That section, so vital, is supported by a post named "vigilance." How is it we have come to believe that once a level of achievement is reached, all is well? "You have it made now!" Often, reaching a certain age has led us to a false assurance that we have arrived! Nothing can overcome us. We have worked hard and long and now we can just turn loose and let go. Well, it is a good idea to let go and let God have his way, but if I understand a great truth of life, and it is throughout God's Word, he is counting on us to be vigilant. Growing older requires more vigilance than less.

On down the fence, in fact, the next post is "tenacity." It looks like a homemade blackgum toothbrush. The top end is worn to a frazzle and the entire post hangs limply on the wire, not in touch with the ground. This post is so close to "vigilance," but it is different. Proclamations that are needed to secure this post will have to do with "stickability." John Warren Steen, former editor of *Mature Living,* has given us a lesson from the lowly, but expensive, postage stamp that may suggest the need for tenacity in our proclamation to senior adults. He shares some verses of unknown origin.

> There was a little postage stamp,
>     No bigger than your thumb;
> But still it stuck right on the job
>     Until its work was done,
> They licked it and pounded it
>     Till it would make you sick;
> But the more it took the lickin'
>     Why, the tighter it would stick.
> Let's be like the little postage stamp
>     In playing life's big game;
> And stick to what we know is right,
>     And we can't miss our aim.[6]

Other sturdy fence posts are needed if we could mend the fences. However, care must be exercised concerning an overemphasis. Such extremes, again, only accentuate the distinctiveness of senior adults until a form of segregation is the result.

Dr. Frank Stagg, the James Buchanan Harrison Professor of New Testament at Southern Baptist Theological Seminary, has spoken most effectively about the beauty and power of aging. He has presented a realistic approach that does not yield to a glorification of age and disparagement of youth. His address delivered at the Southern Baptist Conference on Aging in Nashville, Tennessee, October 23, 1974, provided an outline which may serve as a guideline for new proclamations. The outline which may serve as a guideline for new proclamations. The outline is as follows:

1. Biblical perspectives on age
2. Quality and quantity in life
3. The cult of youth
4. Maturity
5. Senescence
6. Retirement
7. Accepting life in its full cycle

In proclamation "many attitudes are more easily caught by a congregation from its pastor than deliberately taught."[7] His day-to-day messages of life are the most important. Gray and Moberg suggest that proclamations about the importance of independent living, social structures that impede senior adults, and the use of spiritual resources for daily strength as well as in the adjustment crises during aging are needed.[8]

## Educational alterations

Continuing education has become a burgeoning business in the world. The knowledge explosion as well as the increased conviction that we can and must keep on learning are two discernible causes. Another is the gradually dwindling numbers of youth. Senior adults, increasing in numbers and demonstrating learning proficiencies, have created a market that has inspired competition between educational and training institutions.

To reach this growing group and maintain their interest, institutions are altering their teaching methodology. Pedagogy, the art and science of teaching children, has been used since the monastic schools of the twelfth century. Unfortunately, from that century until our time "education has been based upon a set of pedagogical assumptions."[9]

Malcolm S. Knowles, Professor of Adult and Community College Education, North Carolina State University, clarifies the differentiation of a learning theory termed "andragogy" from "pedagogy." He wrote:

In Europe, in the early sixties, adult educators began to feel a need for subsuming this growing body of theory and knowledge about adult learning under a label that would differentiate it from the conventional body of theory called pedagogy, and so they discovered that in 1833 a German adult educator had coined the word, "andragogy," derived from the Greek word "aner" which in ancient Greek meant "man not boy." They had another word for mankind which was "anthropo" but the only word they had for an adult person was "aner." In 1962 in Yugoslavia, the University of Belgrade established a faculty of andragogy that was separate from and in fact at the opposite end of the campus from the faculty of pedagogy. Then a year or two later the University of Zagreb established one, then a couple of years later the University of Amsterdam changed their faculty of pedagogy to the faculty of pedagogy and andragogy. Concordia University, which is a merger of Loyola of Montreal and Sir George Williams in Montreal, established an undergraduate degree program in adragogy and is now about to make it a Masters program. Andragogy is increasingly being accepted as a label for describing this emerging body of theory and derivative practice technology for theory about adult learning.[10]

As I see it, the major educational alteration for senior adults is to gradually shift to a greater use of andragogy, the art and science of helping maturing human beings learn. You will notice that I used the word "gradually," and the words "greater use." Andragogy does appear to be the method of choice to help maturing persons. However, many are dependent and would require a teacher-directed learning situation. Thus, pedagogy is not bad and andragogy good! The individual and the context will determine the appropriate use of these approaches.

Recently, a prominent adult educator shared with me the plight of a traditional English teacher who had returned for doctoral studies. Her new direction was, in the main, adult education. When teaching children she had no compunctions about writing extremely critical remarks across the face of their papers. Such practices were found to be completely unacceptable to mature adult learners. Much more subtle differences result in an ambivalence on the part of many senior adults. Many executives accustomed to being self-directed become dependent in a learning situation. Pedagogues may thrive on this type of dependency relationship and foster it.

Another educational alteration is the provision of a wide selection of learning experiences. In the context of church educational programs this may require a reevaluation of exactly what learning experiences have to do with the development of a maturing Christian. Many of our great, present-day universities began under the sponsorship of religious groups. Also, intergenerational groups should prove to be a helpful alteration. Maybe, as educators, we have created "a supposed gap," and youth and age are really unacquainted.

Does the content need to be altered so that learning experiences may guide and nurture senior adults toward personal satisfaction and fulfillment through service? Consider the isolated homebound person. His inactivity makes learning experiences most valuable in preventing premature mental impairments. This is especially true for those who were, before confinement, active intellectually. The excitement and challenge of new ideas help to keep the mind alert.

## Mend the fences together

The job of mending fences is for all age groups! I have attended some conferences on gerontology where not a single older person was in leadership or a participant. From the mouths of the speakers flowed the beautiful accolades for senior adults—their wisdom, attitudes, intelligence, and so forth. From the plans and programs, I could hear, "We need to help senior adults because they are not wise enough and sufficiently articulate to get the job done." What a contradiction! Neither will we be effective if we give a token nod in their direction because we recognize the above problem. The crucial question is, "Do I believe that senior adults are able to accomplish many laudable tasks with only a minimum of assistance and moral support?" I have viewed films and slides of the Shepherd's Center in Kansas City, one of the outstanding programs for senior adults in America. Senior adults provide a majority of the leadership.

An interesting but disturbing letter speaks to the one-sided leadership that can delay our efforts to build the fences together:

Dear Mr. Roberts:

It is with regret I inform you of my decision to resign from the planning task force for senior adults. As you know I was asked to serve about a year ago as their representative. Because of the opportunity for service to my own age group and indirectly the entire church, I accepted with pleasure.

I attended the first meeting in September. Everyone seemed to be in agreement. I recall little discussion and few questions, although I had many. Two similar monthly meetings followed with only scattered questions and discussions but mainly staff presentations. Several were absent. Because most of us were not aware of the details of what the staff was presenting, I suggested working committees. A motion was made but nothing ever happened. I must admit I enjoyed the luncheon for us but was shocked when I saw the slides of some programs that would soon be initiated. I, nor any of the other planning members, had any input. Since coming on the planning task force we have not had an opportunity to contribute or to do a thorough job of planning. We have been asked to rubber-stamp proposed programs. I cannot conscientiously allow myself to be held responsible. Please accept my resignation.

Sincerely,
JOHN DOE

Unusual rationalizations would be necessary to maintain self-esteem, if older persons were considered unable to plan for themselves. Working together with other age groups who respect their judgment and ability is more beneficial to senior adults than the projects themselves!

There are other places in which we should build the fences together. One place is in our families. Margaret Mead said: "We in America have very little interdependence. The real issue is whether a society keeps its older people close to children and young people. If old people are separated from family life, there is a real tragedy both for them and the young."[11]

Others lament about thousands of college student peers that are packed together in our universities without contact with senior adults. They find themselves in an educational context where they are deprived of life. Contact with peers is important "but when there is no world around you as a reminder of where you came from or where you will go, that closeness might become stagnating instead of mobilizing. And that is a real tragedy.[12]

## Oiling the hinges

Unless senior adults can enter and move freely about in facilities, their incapacities are highlighted and choices limited. Most of us are grateful for the requirements imposed on most builders of new buildings in regard to the handicapped. This group includes a large number of senior adults. Unfortunately, the building codes are not always applicable to old buildings.

Joe J. Jordan, a member of the American Institute of Architects, has prepared a list of exceptional goal statements for all types of facilities where senior adults congregate. The goals are:

1. Increase opportunities for individual choice
2. Minimize dependence and encourage personal independence
3. Reinforce the individual's level of competence (An overdesigned facility with excessive safety aids may threaten self-respect.)
4. Compensate for sensory and perception changes
5. Recognize some decrease in physical mobility
6. Improve comprehension and orientation
7. Encourage social interaction
8. Stimulate participation
9. Provide individual privacy
10. Reduce distractions and conflicts
11. Provide a safe environment
12. Make activities and services accessible
13. Improve the public image of the elderly
14. Plan for growth and change.[13]

In general, the adaptation of church buildings to senior adults has been limited to the attaching of hearing aids to selected pews. Senior adults rarely use them because they are conspicuously close to the front of the sanctuary. The use of nonskid floor wax, accessible restrooms, nonglare lighting, good acoustics, proper heating and cooling, and comfortable pews are only a few of the possible changes that would benefit senior adults.[14]

Older public buildings usually have little if any adaptations made to accommodate older persons. Even the modern buildings are designed more for entrance and movement than for many of the decrements seen in age.

*Jerusalem was mentioned first*

There is a wisdom about the sequence mentioned in Acts 1:8. "But ye shall receive power, after that the Holy Ghost is come upon you: and ye shall be witnesses unto me both in Jerusalem, and in Samaria, and unto the uttermost part of the earth." Maybe it is true that "missions begin at home."

Single adults number forty-eight million in the United States. Of this group twelve million are 65 + .[15] In 1973 a limited study by Eric Pfeiffer revealed that 28 percent of senior adults 65+ lived alone.[16] Thus, approximately six million of the 65 + population live by themselves.

It would be wrong to neglect our emphasis on helping large numbers of people who live at great distances from us. Can we really be missionaries out there unless we are missionaries at home? Senior adults in great need surround our churches. Those in greatest need are not observed because of their isolation. They are "out of sight" and "out of mind."

Twenty-four thousand nursing homes provide unparalled mission opportunities for all age groups, especially senior adults. Now, mission boards and organizations have made it possible for senior adults through partial self-support to be used as mission volunteers.

Government programs are apparently helping senior adults all across our land. State councils on aging and area agencies on aging are throughout the fifty states. Sometimes the citizenry and churches are oblivious of the myriads of services that are available in our communities. A close cooperation of church and community agencies is needed if we would meet the challenge of missions for and through our older Americans.

## Faith That Old Age May Be the Most Beautiful Time of Life

Is it possible that through our studies of aging as development, our faith in the joys of aging may increase? Can we really believe that the "sunset can be more beautiful than the sunrise"?—that aging may be a way into the light rather than into darkness?

Judy Paris wrote graphically of an older couple whom she had observed seated opposite her in a restaurant. She estimated that they had been married for forty or fifty years. But she noticed that they were pensive, not talking, and eating slowly. She wondered about the direction of their thoughts or if they had had a quarrel. They seemed not to notice each other. The thought crossed her mind that possibly the routine, the expected, and repeated phrases had caused life for them to be too familiar and boring.

His wife seemed not to notice anything he was doing, lost still in her own thoughts as her eyes wandered about the room. Yet, she rose from the table in unison with him.

They still did not speak as they pushed their chairs gently toward the table and prepared to leave, she in front of him, he slowly reaching for his cane and holding check and wallet. Just then his knee brushed the corner of a chair and he stumbled, ever so slightly.

"Be careful; be careful, Papa," she said, and her arm reached out should he fall. He was quick to reassure her.

"I'm okay, Mama, let's go," and he slipped his arm around her waist, still clutching his check and wallet.

They moved slowly to the cashier's counter, and I realized that these two were very much together.[17]

Something of a paradox exists in these beautiful observations. Individual differences increase with age but togetherness may be greater than ever before. A poignant lesson is found here, togetherness and individuality are not enemies! Aging offers possibilities for a wedding of these modern-day opposites.

There is much darkness related to aging. And, "in all likelihood, many of the conditions which are the cause of much suffering to the elderly will remain with us for some years to come."[18] But the signs of light are visible in the lives of many senior adults. It is possible to meet an old man with a gentle smile, who suggests that maybe there is more to see than we first thought.[19]

And, behold, there was a man in Jerusalem, whose name was Simeon; and the same man was just and devout, waiting for the consolation of Israel: and the Holy Ghost was upon him. And it was revealed unto him by the Holy Ghost, that he should not see death, before he had seen the Lord's Christ. And he came by the Spirit into the temple: and when the parents brought in the child Jesus, to do for him after the custom of the law, Then took he him up in his arms, and blessed God, and said, Lord, now lettest thou thy servant depart in peace, according to thy word: For mine eyes have seen thy salvation, Which thou hast prepared before the face of all people; A light to lighten the Gentiles, and the glory of the people Israel.[20]

Simeon provides us with a classic example of the possibility of having some of life's greatest experiences even as death is near. Against the bleak backdrop of depressing statistics the Light of the world is brighter than the noonday sun for many senior adults.

## Preparation for Aging

Can one prepare for aging? I asked that question at a public place and received a variety of answers. "You close your eyes and stumble on through." "There is nothing you can do, it just creeps up on you." One man blurted out from a stool over in the corner of the restaurant, "You can be born again like those religious nuts say, whatever that means." I had no idea that a defiant and sarcastic response could contain so great a truth. Out of a new beginning in Christ we would be able to prepare for life and beyond. It is no wonder that the gospel of Christ has been considered such good news! Imagine our being able to have new life, abundant life, and eternal life through him. However, the secret is in giving our lives rather than trying to save them. Possibly the best way to view preparation for aging is to see it as preparation of a life for God.

Preparation for aging should not be equated with tasks designed to merely give quantity to life. Quantity and quality are not always coextensive. The years of Christ's earthly life covered a brief span but his aging and death were prepared before the foundation of the worlds. His life was given!

The life and death of Christ should further inform us about a partner-ship in our preparation for aging. The initial preparation in the most important phase is begun when we begin our journey with him. It is not a solo flight as you would think if you subscribed fully to the human potential movement. "Growth for a Christian is based on dependence and commitment. These are not attitudinal positions espoused by the human potentialists. In fact, dependence would have all the earmarks of immaturity."[21] Yes, preparation that insures successful aging is when one is informed by Christ. Is this a destructive dependency? Can I not choose the resources and truths that would be most helpful in my living a life for him? Thus, preparation is not a self-centered preoccupation but a sharing and doing of God's will. God gives good returns—abundant life.

Preparation for aging may be described as "preparation for maturity" or "preparation for development of one's potential." Aging, described as maturity, is seen as directional and is beyond human attainment. The New Testament word for this goal means literally *completion,* and is translated as *perfection* in the King James Version, and as *maturity* in the Revised Standard Version. Maturity is defined in Ephesians as "the measure of the stature of the fulness of Christ," and the reader is encouraged to "grow up into him in all things, which is the head, even Christ" (Eph. 4:13,15).[22]

Preparation for aging includes a destiny that moves beyond earthly existence. In fact, eternity began at the moment of union with Christ. Glenn H. Asquith shares some meaningful thoughts as we contemplate preparation for completion in his "Top of the Mountain."

> The slope to be climbed is climbed,
> The upward struggle is past;
> The growing pains are stilled;
> The mined treasure is garnered.
>
> Now, on top of the mountain,
> For the moment aimless,
> The retired person stands.
> What is left to do?

Chattering he may boast of height achieved,
Of how fiercely he strove,
What agonies he suffered,
Sum up the possessions at his feet.

Or, he may turn to find
Not an effortless slide down the other side,
But a slender stairway
Inviting to heights of the Spirit.[23]

This is a Christian psychology of aging. Life that began by him, must be sustained and nurtured through him, and brought to completion and full maturity with him, forever!

"Lord, help to make our last years on earth our best years as we offer them to thee."

## NOTES

[1]Thomas Gordon, *Parent Effectiveness Training* (New York: Peter H. Wyden, Inc., 1970), pp. 194-215.

[2]Simone de Beauvoir, *The Coming of Age* (New York: C. P. Putnam's Sons, 1972), p. 77.

[3]Tournier, *Learn to Grow Old*, p. 169.

[4]Ibid., p. 217.

[5]Ethel Sabin Smith, *Dynamics of Aging* (New York: W. W. Norton & Company, Inc., 1956), p. 115.

[6]John Warren Steen, "A Lesson from a Stamp," *Mature Living* 3 (January 1979)4:4.

[7]Robert M. Gray and David O. Moberg, *The Church and the Older Person*, rev. ed. (Grand Rapids: Wm. B. Eerdmans Publishing Company, 1977), p. 190.

[8]Ibid.

[9]Malcolm S. Knowles, "Adult Learning Processes: Pedagogy and Andragogy," *Religious Education* 72 (March-April 1977)2:202.

[10]Ibid., pp. 205-206.

[11]Grace Hechinger, "Interview with Margaret Mead," *Family Circle* (July 26, 1977), p. 27.

[12]Nouwen and Gaffney, *Aging*, p. 120.

[13]Joe J. Jordan, "Facility Design: First, a Supportive Environment," *Perspective on Aging* 7 (March-April 1978)2:33-34.

[14]Gray and Moberg, *The Church and the Older Person*, p. 169.

[15]Nicolas B. Christoff, *Saturday Night, Sunday Morning* (San Francisco: Harper & Row, 1978), pp. 1-2.

[16]Pfeiffer, "Psychopathology," p. 266.

[17]Judy Paris, "Very Much Together," *Home Life* (October 1974), p. 9.

[18]Nouwen and Gaffney, *Aging*, p. 51.

[19]Ibid.

[20]Luke 2:25-32.

[21]William E. Hulme, *Your Potential Under God* (Minneapolis, Minn.: Augsburg Publishing House, 1978), pp. 131-32.

[22]Ibid., p. 131.

[23]Glenn H. Asquith, *Living Creatively as an Older Adult* (Scottsdale, Pa.: Herald Press, 1975), p. 180.